MOTHER TERESA'S

Lessons of Love & Secrets of Sanctity

MOTHER TERESA'S

Lessons of Love & Secrets of Sanctity

✎ Susan Conroy

Our Sunday Visitor Publishing Division
Our Sunday Visitor, Inc.
Huntington, Indiana 46750

Our Sunday Visitor Publishing Division
Our Sunday Visitor, Inc.
200 Noll Plaza
Huntington, IN 46750

ISBN: 1-931709-76-9 (Inventory No. T42)
LCCN: 2003100091

Cover design by Monica Haneline
Cover photos (front and back) of Mother Teresa by Catholic News Service; used with permission. Photo (back cover) of Susan Conroy and Mother Teresa provided by the author. Unless otherwise noted, photos provided by the author; all photos are used with permission.

Interior design by Sherri L. Hoffman

I love you, Mother Teresa.

You are still right here in my heart.

Table of Contents

Introduction

When I arrived at Mother Teresa's doorstep in Calcutta, India, for the first time in 1986, I knew in my heart that what I was about to experience would impact the rest of my life — but I did not have any idea how much. What I witnessed in Mother Teresa alone was enough to alter the course of my life: instead of pursuing a lucrative career in the corporate world, I longed simply to continue helping people. My experiences with her gave me a deeper understanding of what life is all about; they made me cherish my Christian faith even more; and they led me to discover a depth of joy and fulfillment that I had never felt before.

I had a very simple dream when I made my first journey to India: I hoped that I could lighten the suffering of even just *one* human being while I was there. I also wished, with all my heart, to have a chance to sit in a dark corner of the Home for the Dying and simply *lay eyes on* Mother Teresa, even for just a few minutes, as she was shining her love on others. Believing so deeply that she was a living saint, I longed to see her love in action and to learn all that I could from her. I was able not only to *see* her, but also to speak with her, to pray with her, and to hold her hand. I was able to help her care for orphans and for the dying in her shelters, to make drawings and paintings for her at her own request, to correspond with her by letter throughout the years, and now to share with others her lessons of love.

Mother Teresa had welcomed anyone with "hands to serve and a heart to love" to join her in ministering to the Poorest of the Poor. Once I accepted her invitation, I began caring for AIDS patients for the first time. I came in contact with men and women with leprosy, and I witnessed death for the first time in my life — at an unforgettably close range. The impact of these experiences on my life has been remarkable and ongoing, as these pages will reveal.

Mother Teresa's life was inseparable from her faith. Her entire life's work was founded on these words which Jesus Christ spoke: "For I was hungry and you gave me food, I was thirsty and you gave me drink, I was a stranger and you welcomed me, I was naked and you clothed me, I was sick and you visited me, I was in prison and you came to me…. Truly, I say to you, as you did it to one of the least of these my brethren, you did it to me" (Mt 25:35-36, 40).

Mother Teresa took Jesus at His Word. She taught us that in serving the hungry, the unloved and the rejected, we were serving Jesus "in His distressing disguise of the poor." She took my hand one day and, pointing to each of my outstretched fingers, she explained that whenever we reach out to those who are suffering on the streets, whenever we touch the patients in the Home for the Dying, we should remember these five words that Jesus spoke: "You did it to me" (Mt 25:40), and then we should go about touching, serving, and caring for each person with the same tenderness, humility, love, and reverence with which we would touch and serve Jesus Christ Himself. She taught us that in serving the poor, we were directly serving God.

It is quite meaningful to me that the very first words I ever read by Mother Teresa were given to me by my own mother, and they were words on Joy: "Joy is prayer. Joy is strength. Joy is love…."

Mother Teresa spoke even more beautifully about joy by her *example*. Her smile was enough to set hearts aflame with incredible happiness. Being in her presence was like receiving a spiritual injection! Her co-workers could then go out into the worst slums of Calcutta and face the worst human suffering with inner strength and an incessant smile. As we were returning to work at the Home for the Dying after visiting with her one day, a volunteer friend of mine looked at me and said: "Susan, you're *shining* again!" It was the result of being in Mother Teresa's presence.

Mother Teresa encouraged me to, "Find ways to make others happy. Life is the joy of loving and being loved." She taught me the infinite value of "little things": giving water to someone who is thirsty; holding an orphan who is crying; reaching out to someone who is lonely. She said: "Let no one ever come to you without leaving better and happier." One day while I was caring for a man in the Home for the Dying, this man suddenly became peaceful and quiet in my arms, and I realized that he had died while I was holding him. I had never experienced this before and I was so touched by it that I began to cry. Mother Teresa came right to my side and helped me to close his eyes, fold his hands and take care of him. I did not do any *great* things for this man. I simply held him and did my best to love him. And yet, in spite of the littleness of my deeds, Mother Teresa looked into my eyes and said: "You have received many graces for this." I learned that God looks into our hearts to see the value of our deeds. We are not necessarily called to do great things in the world. Only "small things with great love."

Mother Teresa had so many powerfully inspiring qualities — her radiance of joy, profound humility, rock-solid faith, an intense spiritual life. One day, I went into her chapel at the Motherhouse to pray all alone. Soon after entering the chapel, I noticed that Mother Teresa was there, kneeling all by herself on the floor in deep prayer. In all my life, I will never forget the sight of her that day — the visible radiance of love in her lowered face as she knelt there alone on the floor. It was such a deep communion with God. So obvious to me was her direct contact with heaven that I felt like tapping her on the shoulder and saying, "Please give Him my love while you have Him on the line!"

There was also her obvious selflessness, single-heartedness, a great sense of humor, and a tremendous love of God. No one carried Jesus quite the way she did. It was powerfully moving to watch her carry the Blessed Sacrament to and from the Tabernacle before and after Adoration. The intense love, humility, and tenderness with which she held the Precious Body of Christ close to her heart would make you cry. It left a great impression on each one of us who witnessed it. It delights me endlessly that now Our Lord can embrace her and press her close to *His* Heart. They say imitation is the greatest form of flattery. This would be the most beautiful way for us to pay tribute to Mother Teresa — by imitating her tremendous love for God and her goodness to others, each in our own special way.

On Friday, September 5, 1997, when news of Mother Teresa's passing spread throughout the world, I received a call from my friend Paul in Paris whom I had met while working with Mother Teresa in Calcutta. He had been very close to her, and rather than feeling despair at this recent news, his voice was full of hope. "This is so special," he said. "We can pray to Mother Teresa now." In my own heart, I felt a deep sense of peace and joy. I know that Mother Teresa is unspeakably happy now. She had truly longed for heaven where God is — and she is in heaven with Him now — with Him Whom she loved so intensely in this life. And I think that our relationship with Mother Teresa can be even closer now. All of us can be near her. Calcutta is very far away from us. Heaven is a lot closer. Mother Teresa is only a prayer away. I know that her work of love will continue, because, as she always said, it is truly "*God's* work."

When she was only eighteen years old, Mother Teresa took her religious name after young Saint Thérèse of Lisieux, the "Little Flower." In September 1997, the Catholic Church celebrated the 100th anniversary of when Saint Thérèse herself entered into heaven, the same month in which Mother Teresa was called home to God. Just before entering into eternal life, the Little Flower said, "I want to spend my heaven doing good on earth." She did not want to just sit back and enjoy eternal rest. I know that Mother Teresa was not one to rest either. Somehow I can imagine these two saints, Mother Teresa and little Saint Thérèse, side by side in heaven, showering us all with "roses," with special favors, and continuing to do so much good in the world. May we share this work *with* them by doing our part to spread the fragrance of God's love everywhere on earth.

May we give heartfelt *thanks* and *praise* to God for Mother Teresa — for the wonderful gift of inspiration and love that she has been to us.

At the end of my last letter to Mother Teresa, which she received just weeks before her death, I wrote the same sentiments that I wish to say to her today: "Thank you with all my heart for your love and prayers. God bless you every day, dearest Mother ... I love you."

(Excerpt from the eulogy I delivered at the memorial service for Mother Teresa at the Cathedral of the Immaculate Conception in Portland, Maine, on September 10, 1997 — the 51st anniversary of the day Mother Teresa received her inspiration from Jesus "to serve Him among the Poorest of the Poor.")

Photo courtesy of the Missionaries of Charity

Mother Teresa of Calcutta

MISSIONARIES of CHARITY
54 A, A.J.C. BOSE ROAD
CALCUTTA 700016 INDIA
6 August 1996

Susan Conroy
18 Spruce Lane
Gorham, Maine 04038
U.S.A.

Dear Susan,

Thank you for your letter and the article
you wrote on your drawing of the little
child in the Hand of God.

How great is the humility of God to use
people like you and me to bring His love
and compassion to those who are suffering.
Let us thank God for allowing us to be
channels of His love.

Yes, you may write about your experiences
in Calcutta. Let it be for the glory of
God. Entrust yourself to the Immaculate
Heart of Mary and ask her to be a mother
to you.

Let us pray.

God Bless you
M. Teresa mc

This is the letter Mother Teresa sent to me giving me permission to write this book. She signed her letters, "God Bless you. M. Teresa, M.C." (Missionaries of Charity). In the top left-hand corner of her letters, she used to put a small cross with the letters "LDM." This comes from the Latin phrase *Laudetur Deo Mariaeque*, meaning "Praise to God and to Mary."

Foreword

❧

$\mathcal{I}$ have always felt that my personal experiences with Mother Teresa and her Missionaries of Charity in India were a gratuitous gift from God, and they were meant to be shared.

Typically, my sharing is done in the form of slide presentations. In 1996, after speaking to a corporate audience about my first journey to Calcutta, I was told that it changed people's perspectives on life, that people could relate to it in their own personal lives, and that they were starving to hear more about God and about the spiritual lessons I learned. One person wrote "even an atheist" could see Someone was moving me to make this journey. "Like most people, I am constantly in search of experiences that will deepen my faith and enrich my spirituality," another person wrote. "Your story has without question been one of the most enriching I have experienced...."

These responses inspired me to find a way to share this experience with as many people as possible. I wrote to Mother Teresa and asked her for permission to write this book. I explained to her that my writing was not very fancy and it would not win any literary prizes. "It would be like a love story," I told her, "filled with joy and many of the lessons that I learned." Just *days* after I had asked her for permission to write this book, she wrote her response.

Mother Teresa counseled me to write my story "for God's glory and for the good of souls." On several occasions, she told me to undertake this project "with Jesus and for Jesus." She also encouraged me to entrust myself "to the Immaculate Heart of Mary" and to ask her to be a mother to me as I wrote these pages. I have tried my very best to do all of these things, just as Mother Teresa requested. I have earnestly prayed that God's spirit of love and truth would grace these pages, illuminate my thoughts, and guide my pen. I have longed for this book to be truly pleasing to God, like a hymn of praise and thanksgiving for all that He has done. And I have been filled with a constant wish that Mother Teresa will know by these pages how much I love her.

These pages are filled with the precious words of Mother Teresa. Many a time I stood near her as she spoke with wisdom, joy, and love to young volunteers from every corner of the earth who, like me, longed to see her and to learn from her. In recounting my experiences with Mother, and with her permission, I drew upon many public and private sources of her words to help enrich the story. Many of these are noted throughout the text, and all are listed at the end of this book.

With all my heart, I wish to dedicate this book above all to God and to the Immaculate Heart of Mary, Whom Mother Teresa taught me to love and trust beyond all telling.

Part I

My Dream of Going to India

Chapter One

✣

All Things Are Possible

*S*aint Thomas à Kempis said: "Love never sees anything as impossible, for it believes everything is possible and everything is permitted." When we love, we are always filled with hope for miracles, for "nothing is impossible with God." When I first began dreaming of going to Calcutta and working with Mother Teresa in her Home for the Dying, I never imagined that it was impossible. I simply thought it might take a while for this wish to come true.

How the Dream Began

I was a student at Dartmouth College. That, in and of itself, is very significant, for the atmosphere at Dartmouth is like a fairy tale, conducive to dreaming and to believing that anything is possible. Nestled in the beautiful valley of Hanover, New Hampshire, with breathtaking mountains and flowing rivers hugging the campus, we students felt as if we were in an earthly paradise; and, as remote as it might seem to the

Dartmouth Hall, Dartmouth College.

noise and activities of the world, the world was, practically speaking, our classroom. Opportunities and possibilities for learning and personal growth were as endless as our imaginations. Although my career plans at that time were to enter the corporate world and my studies were concentrated in Economics, my deepest personal interests were in matters of the heart and the spirit, in the "science of love," so to speak. These personal interests led me to the doorstep of Mother Teresa of Calcutta, a living saint. My journey to India was the fruit of a gradual blossoming of inspiring and totally unforeseen happenings. It was the working of grace more than a carefully planned course of events.

My mother used to write to me very often while I was away at college. As I walked back to my dormitory room one day during my sophomore year, I opened an envelope from her and discovered something surprising inside. It was a page from a magazine with a brightly colored painting of Mother Teresa with her hands folded in prayer, and it included some beautiful words by Mother Teresa about JOY. These words impressed me as soon as I read them:

> JOY is prayer. Joy is strength. Joy is love — Joy is the net of love by which we can catch souls. We give most when we give with joy. The best way to show our gratitude to God and to each other is to accept everything with joy. A joyful heart is the inevitable result of a heart burning with love.
>
> We all long for heaven where God is, but we have it in our power to be in heaven with Him right now — to be happy with Him at this very moment. But being happy with Him now means:
> loving as He loves,
> helping as He helps,
> giving as He gives,
> serving as He serves,
> rescuing as He rescues,
> being with Him for all the twenty-four hours, and
> touching Him in His distressing disguise of the poor.

These were the *very first words* I ever read by Mother Teresa. When I got back to my room, I taped this piece of paper up on my wall, and I found great inspiration in reading these words time and time again. The simplicity, beauty, and truth in them were very appealing to me — and yet, as meaningful as these words were to me at that time, it never occurred to me that one day I would meet Mother Teresa and be close to her beloved poor. (Please see the illustration in the color photo section.)

From time to time, my mother would order religious books for our family. She was the most peaceful, happy, patient, and loving mother any child could ever hope for, and she nourished us with good things in every way. I benefited greatly from these books, because my heart was always inclined toward God and holy things. I am one of ten children. My parents raised our family in the Roman Catholic tradition and they lived their faith beautifully. They kept us very close to God and to the sacraments while we were growing up — we attended Mass on Sundays, and we went to confession every two weeks. We often prayed together as a family at night, kneeling before a beautiful big painting of Our Lady holding the Divine Child on her lap, and most memorably on Christmas morning, before rushing downstairs to open presents. In the mornings, while we were all getting ready for school or work, my father always questioned us — "Did you say your prayers?" My parents always referred to us as their "ten treasures," and the most important thing my father taught us was to "keep the faith," so that all of his treasures would arrive safely in heaven in the end.

While home from college on break several months after receiving the special enclosure on "JOY," I came across a set of three small books on the living room coffee table, which my mother had purchased for our family. They were written by Mother Teresa.[1] I began to read, first one, and then another. I absorbed every word, like a thirsty flower soaking up the refreshing rain. In those little books I learned about the suffering and wretched poverty in Calcutta. I also learned that Mother Teresa was like a bright light amid that darkness of human misery. As I read about the need for "hands to serve and a heart to love," I remember looking down at my hands and thinking: "I have two strong hands; maybe I can help her to hold some of the orphans in the Children's Home. I have my health and strength and joy; maybe I can feed and comfort some of the patients in the Home for the Dying. I have a peaceful and happy heart; maybe I can bring joy to the people who are suffering there." Mother Teresa made it sound so simple. She made it sound as if all one needs are hands and a heart and what she called "a joyful willingness to do even the most humble work for the sick and dying."

This is how the dream began.

I deeply desired to be in the presence of Mother Teresa *someday*. If only I could see her and touch her. If only I could hear her speak. If only I could work alongside her and learn all that I could from this living saint. I considered how wonderful and blessed it would be to have the opportunity to watch, to work alongside, and to learn from Mother Teresa, who lived such an exemplary life. I wanted to see her, if only for a moment. I wanted to see Christ so beautifully reflected and alive in another human being — to see our own *potential*, to learn all that I could by watching and listening to someone who embodies Christ's own Spirit, His own qualities, to such a degree that it would seem as though I were witnessing Christ Himself walking the earth once again and showing us all the path of selfless love. I believe in making what is ideal *real*. A peaceful, more loving, more beautiful world was ideal in my eyes. With the examples of Mother Teresa, of Christ Himself, and even of my mother, I could see that we have the means to make ideals come true, to make the world a little more perfect. With their beautiful examples, I wanted to learn how to nurture Christ in myself and in others. I thought about how I would love to witness and learn Mother Teresa's ways *firsthand* and thereby witness Christ's ways. We were so blessed to have Mother Teresa walking the earth in our own time, teaching us what we ourselves can be.

This book, in large part, is about how dreams come true.

It Was Like a Seed Planted in My Heart

If you find a dream inside your heart, don't ever let it go. For dreams can be the tiny seeds from which tomorrows grow.
AUTHOR UNKNOWN

Mother Teresa said that "God proves straightaway what He really wants by the results. The most important thing is to pray and pray and pray, to see which [path] will produce the greatest good."[2]

After reading the three little books, I was filled with a deep desire to go to Calcutta and offer my hands and heart in ministering to the

Poorest of the Poor with Mother Teresa. Specifically, I wanted to help those who were suffering in the Home for the Dying. I kept this longing quiet in my heart for some time, not daring to tell anyone about it, because I did not think anyone would understand. I did not know how to explain it, except to say that this dream was like *a seed planted in my heart by God*. This much I knew for sure: I did not place it there myself! I had always loved what was familiar and beautiful to me. This desire to go so far away, to such a radically different culture, far from all that I loved, and to face the complete unknown all by myself was not the sort of dream one might expect of a college girl of twenty.

When I finally opened up about my dream, I encountered opposition. I was told frightful things about Calcutta, and yet the "seed" kept growing stronger and stronger. It would not go away. Whenever I heard dreadful stories about what I would encounter if I were to make the journey, fear came to my heart. But it always subsided. Eventually this fear was replaced by an ever-growing earnestness to serve Christ in His distressing disguise of the poor. As I came to realize more fully that this was not simply my dream, it was *God's* dream for me, I said "yes" in my heart. I was encouraged by the realization that every imagined "fruit" which might come from this experience and every motivation going into it were *all good*. It was very pure and simple. It seemed like a gift and a precious treasure to hold onto, until the time came when the seed would be given all the sunshine and rain it needed to blossom.

Mother Teresa said: "Vocation is like a little seed — it has to be nourished. You have to keep on looking after it. Vocation cannot be forced. It has to come from above. The person whom Christ has chosen for Himself — she knows. Maybe she doesn't know how to express it, but she knows."[3]

I Thought of It as a "Distant Dream"

If you have built castles in the air, your work need not be lost; that is where they should be. Now put the foundations under them.
HENRY DAVID THOREAU

Beautiful Saint Thérèse of Lisieux taught me in her writings that "God cannot inspire unrealizable desires." I had confidence that the dream in my heart was possible. Being realistic, however, I believed that it would be many years before I would ever be able to make this wish come true. Thus, my desire became a distant dream, since I had no means of pursuing it at that time. I was a college student with no extra spending money. I imagined that I would first have to graduate from Dartmouth, get a good job, earn a great salary, and save a sizable amount of income before I could send myself to Calcutta to work as a volunteer. But the dream came true much sooner than I ever imagined possible. Where there's God's will, there's a way. "If we only let Him do it!" Mother Teresa said, "We have only to let Jesus do it — and He does it in a beautiful way!"[4]

I treasured my dream in secret and pondered it in the silence of my heart for a number of weeks. The first person I told about it was my mother. I confided in her, saying, "What would you think if, after graduation, I went to Calcutta and helped Mother Teresa to serve the poor in the Home for the Dying?" She responded immediately, earnestly, and unforgettably. "That would be my worst nightmare!" she said. My dream was virtually laid to waste by her response. Looking back, I realize her reaction was completely natural. The last thing in the world any loving mother would want would be for her young daughter go alone to the other side of the world, to an enormous city filled with poverty, suffering, and danger — especially when this daughter did not speak a word of the native languages and would be exposed to so many diseases as she worked in a Home for the Dying. For these reasons and more, my mother was utterly devastated that I would even *imagine* doing such a thing, and I was upset that *she* was upset! I only wanted to help people, not to hurt anyone in the process — especially not my dear mother. I tried to put aside my dream, but within a short time, my yearning to serve the poor in India came back, in full force, and continued to grow. This is how I knew *most* clearly that it was God's will and not my own. I would never have pursued something that left my parents in great fear for my life unless I sensed clearly and strongly that I was being drawn to make the journey. I knew that, truly, this was a seed planted in my heart by God.

I thank God for my mother. It was my mother who gave me those first words I ever read by Mother Teresa (on joy), and it was she who had ordered the beautiful set of three little books by Mother Teresa which inspired me with such longing. Yet, when I shared this dream

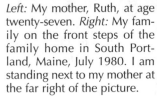

Left: My mother, Ruth, at age twenty-seven. *Right:* My family on the front steps of the family home in South Portland, Maine, July 1980. I am standing next to my mother at the far right of the picture.

with my mother, she could not accept it. Obviously, she had no idea what these letters and books were inspiring in me. She did not realize at the time that God was using her as an instrument of grace and a channel of divine influence in my life. If she had foreseen the consequences of her deeds, namely, the wishes that they would inspire in my heart, I imagine that she would never have followed through with them! It was obviously not her intention to make me dream of helping Mother Teresa someday. It was simply God's intention.

The Future Came Quickly

The future is not in our hands. We have no power over it.... Allow the good God to make plans for the future — for yesterday has gone, tomorrow has not yet come and we have only today to make Him known, loved, and served. Our Lord told us not to fret about tomorrow, which is in God's Hands. So, do not worry about it.

MOTHER TERESA

Allow God to make future plans, Mother Teresa said. He will show you what to do.

After Christmas break, I went back to Dartmouth. It was the spring of 1986, and this dream of mine was quietly placed on a back burner in my heart. I had completely and serenely surrendered to the fact that it had to remain a distant dream. Then one day I came across an article in a college newsletter about how the Tucker Foundation at Dartmouth assists students in reaching out and serving those in need. The article was entitled "Service and Personal Growth." Believing that my wish to care for the poor in India was a perfect match with their objectives, I marched over to the Tucker Foundation's office to speak directly with the associate dean, Jan Tarjan. I asked if they would sponsor me in going to Calcutta to volunteer in Mother Teresa's Home for the Dying. Jan seemed stunned by my proposal. She explained to me that the Foundation did not have a fellowship program for what I was hoping to do. They had never before sent a student to Calcutta on that type of mission. Rather than reject my idea, however, she explained to me that if I could somehow establish contacts in India and set up my own program, I could at least go through the process of applying for funding.

Astonishingly, within a matter of nine weeks, I was on a flight to India with the whole journey paid for by the Tucker Foundation.

As this extraordinary dream crystallized into a beautiful real-life experience, I kept a diary of my emotions, thoughts and activities:

April 26, 1986: *This whole surge of activity (designing my own program to serve the destitute and dying) in some respects seems like a stab in the dark, like a mission impossible with so many arrangements to make and strings to pull, and so little time. But I have so little to lose (besides sleep and study-time!) and so very much to gain should things work out.... This would be, without a doubt, one of the most priceless, challenging, productive, and beautiful experiences of my lifetime.*

April 27, 1986: *My life has been quite free of hardship and filled with an abundance of love. I owe it to someone out there, I owe it to myself, and I owe it to God to suffer for the welfare of others, to develop my potential to love those in need and to light up lives as mine has been so steadily and unfalteringly lighted up by others and by God. I do not want this deep inner feeling ever to die. I do not want this dream to fade. It is very strong — sometimes overpowering — to the point that it is a driving force in my life. I want to be with Mother Teresa herself, whom I admire and respect deeply. Like my own mother, she has so very much to offer in the way of valuable teachings and she is a beautiful example to follow. I would love simply to watch her and learn all I could.*

I think I could return to the U.S.A. and carry this experience with me throughout the rest of my life.

I have been blessed with an ability to see and find beauty in life, in others, in nature. I want to strengthen and develop this. I want to find beauty and share love in the midst of hardship, suffering, and death. I want to be able to bring light into others' lives just as others almost incessantly bring light into mine. I somehow feel that this is my purpose in life. Loving others is what brings mean- ing *and* depth *to my life. This experience will teach me to love others better, to love with more effort, to love with more heart and soul. This experience will enrich my life and the lives of others....*

May 23, 1986: *Why am I going? Why do I want to give up my secure lifestyle and leave everything and everyone I know and love behind? Why do I want to embrace such a devastating, distressing situation? I could go on and on about my attraction to Mother Teresa's depth of life, joy, and love; about my desire to meet this tremendous challenge and draw from it all of its priceless value; about my* desire *to become selfless and giving and to experience something which will impress me so deeply as to remind me every day of my life of where I am going. To be honest, these are indeed my inner feelings, but I am not exactly sure why on earth I am doing something as drastic as this. I love to set my sights high, but this does seem to be going a bit overboard! Nevertheless, it is in my heart — it has a stronghold and cannot be ignored. This will undoubtedly be the most dangerous and the most valuable thing I will ever do in my life. I want to do it. I am not exactly sure why, but I feel that I will know why upon returning home to my loved ones in the United States. I am not exactly certain what I will learn, but I am sure that I will learn and see and do some immeasurably valuable things that I will never forget as long as I live.*

My mood became reflective and sober as I pondered what was about to take place. In my diary, after receiving my acceptance letter from the Tucker Foundation at Dartmouth, I wrote:

May 23, 1986: *I am virtually on my way to Calcutta, India now. I am finding it difficult to believe, and I will not fully believe it until I touch someone in the Home for the Dying.*

I am afraid only that I might not live up to my aspirations and my potential. I do not want to let myself down. I know that I will be very ashamed and disappointed with myself if I react in a negative way to the situation that I am embracing from afar. God, please do not let me be repulsed by the broken, bruised, and grotesque bodies I will undoubtedly see. Please do not let me become paralyzed or withdrawn or depressed. I am not going to Calcutta to be a burden to others or to be useless. Please, God, do not let me see the bodies of the poor as frightful monsters; let me instead see past the outward, unbearable appearances and let me recognize You, my dear Lord — even as beloved Mother Teresa does — in Your distressing disguise. 'God, help me to love You in others with all that I am. Help me to be unafraid as I reach out — with a heart burning with love, just as it is now.

I know that I can do it. I also know that Yours is the only shoulder I will have to lean on. I ask simply that You stay with me, remain here at my side every step of the way.

For twenty years now, my cup has more than overflowed. I cannot even begin to count all of my blessings. God has always given me what I need and so much more. Why should He cease to do so when I need Him most, as I pass through the most trying times of my life? He will be right by my side every step of the way. I know this, and this gives me the strength I need. I am not afraid.

Preparing for the Journey

Do not let your heart be troubled; believe in God....
JOHN 14:1

"Mother said that if she knew what lay ahead when God called her, she would have hesitated," one of her religious Sisters recalled with a smile. "Humanly speaking, you cannot explain it," she said. "In spite of our weakness and our poverties, there are no worries for us, because we know somehow, some way, things will be all right." I could have said these same things about my own journey into the unknown world of suffering and poverty in India.

Naturally, there was fear in my heart at times. Some of my fellow students at Dartmouth were from India, and I would visit them and listen carefully to all that they told me about what to expect in Calcutta. I wanted to learn everything I could about what I was about to face. Virtually all of the students I spoke with tried to discourage me from going. They told me dreadful things about the city. I asked one young Indian student if there was anything encouraging or hopeful that he could tell me. Staring straight into my eyes, he answered: "Don't die over there." His words stunned me. This remark was the only "positive" thing he could say to me about Calcutta.

I was very seriously warned about the overwhelming multitudes of people, the widespread sickness and death, the extreme poverty, the food contamination, the debilitating language barrier, and the general high degree of risk involved in going to live and work in Calcutta. One Indian student warned me that I would be in great danger of being raped, kidnapped, and murdered, and I was very shaken by his words.

Even with all of the dark, frightful pictures painted in my mind, I still wanted to live the dream. That's how I knew something greater than my weak self was prodding and pushing me to take this step of faith. It was not human nature to want to do this, to let go of a secure, comfortable, and protected life to go to a place like Calcutta. I was putting myself into God's Hands alone; I was entrusting my life to Him.

There was a professor in the Government Department at Dartmouth who was quite acclimated to Indian culture. He was like a gift from heaven. Professor Howard Erdman gave me very helpful, practical advice. He enlightened me about typical summer weather conditions in Calcutta and suggested that I bring at least a few light cotton t-shirts; the temperatures would be so high and the humidity so unbearable that I would have to change my clothes a few times a day because I would be drenched with sweat. He warned me to be careful of the drinking water, which in most cases was highly contaminated. He also advised me to watch a particular documentary film on Calcutta, which he warned me was very disturbing. I did view the film, and he was right: it was very troubling indeed! It was also tremendously helpful in preparing me for the reality of my dream.

One of my most valuable and powerful sources of preparation came from a little brown book filled with black and white photographs by Mary Ellen Mark, an extremely gifted photographer from New York. A friend of mine at Dartmouth discovered that I was planning to volunteer in Mother Teresa's Home for Dying Destitutes in Calcutta. He came to me and offered this precious book of photographs of this exact shelter. To this day, I am deeply grateful for his kindness and his saving deed. I experienced an incredible sense of shock and revulsion as I looked at page after page of human agony and death. I had never seen this degree of suffering before. I struggled to look at the photographs of the emaciated bodies of the poor in the very place where I was about to go and serve. I forced myself to look at those pages every day, hoping that in doing so I would not be so frightened when I saw these things in real life. Soon I discovered in the photographs a sense of grace and beauty amid the horrible reality of human suffering in Calcutta. This book of photographs prepared me as nothing else could for what I was about to encounter in India. My friend had given me the book not to encourage me to follow my dream, but in an effort to make me re-think my decision; however, God was using him as an instrument of His grace and goodness, preparing me for this journey of love.

I made a list of things that I hoped to accomplish while I was in Calcutta:

- Volunteer my hands and heart to Mother Teresa's Missionaries of Charity.
- Find and touch each day the broken, bruised body of Christ "in His most distressing disguise" of the poor.

- Work closely with the homeless, abandoned, impoverished, sick, and dying people in the struggling city of Calcutta, India.
- Give a genuine gift of self to those who are most in need.
- Work alongside Mother Teresa, actively trying to learn her ways of selfless devotion, love, and joyful service to the unwanted and the dying.
- Grow stronger in faith (believing in myself, and believing in God).
- Grow stronger in love, compassion, and sensitivity to those who are suffering near me.
- Grow in appreciation for what I have been given.
- Grow in concern for human life.
- Grow in my ability to help others, to sense needs, to respond to those needs, and to deal well with suffering and death.
- Carry through life all that I have and will learn, and to share this with others.
- Always feel the impact of this experience with the destitute, abandoned, homeless, unwanted, sick, and dying in Calcutta.

"Don't Be Too Trusting"

In contrast to the discouraging words I was told about Calcutta by my classmates, so much love and support came to me from my closest friends, my brothers and sisters, and my uncles and aunts when the dream started coming true and I was making final preparations for my journey to India.

"Promise to take care of yourself as you serve God and others this coming summer," wrote my friend, Mrs. Pelikan. "I wish I could go with you, because that's what life is all about. Each one of us *can* make a difference in this world for the poor, the sick and the homeless, because we *are* our brother's keeper. I pray for you to be strong and can't wait to hear all about your experiences. Our love and prayers go with you. With God's peace and joy.… "

It was most difficult for my parents. Telling Mom and Dad, and seeing their reactions, was most painful. Mom was utterly distraught by the news and she became withdrawn, in a way that I had never seen before in my life. She was silent for three days. Papa was supportive but filled with concern. I remember so clearly that as I was preparing to leave, he told me, "Don't be too trusting." My father knew that I was friendly, open, and trusting of others. This could get me into a great deal of danger! His words of advice would ring clearly in my mind during my long journey across the world to India.

Having courage did not mean that I had no heartache over the upcoming journey. There was plenty of heartache when the time came for me to leave home. I never dreamed that it would be quite so heart-breaking. I never dreamed that I would cause so very much pain. My father called it by another name: *Love.*

Papa said, "I fear." Whenever we spoke about my upcoming jour-ney, tears came to his eyes, he got all choked up, and I broke down as well. He knew that I was my own person, with my own mind and will. He respected me for doing what I felt that I had to do. But he was very much afraid for me. Every single time he expressed his fear, tears welled in his eyes. He understood so well that I was going along with what was inside of me. I would not undertake such a frightening thing if it were not so deeply implanted in my heart and soul.

Mama's reaction hurt the most. It hurt so much to see her sorrow and heartache, and to know that I was causing it. I don't think I ever cried so much in such a short time as I did on the night I broke the news to her that I was going to India. I think I utterly broke her heart. She said she could not accept it; she could not accept my going to such a hideous place in India. She could not let me go again, after such a sorrowful, difficult separation the previous year when I had studied in Arles, France. She could not accept another enormous burden after all of those in the recent past (she had been diagnosed with cancer several months earlier), which just had to be absorbed without a whimper. She could not let go after all our dreams and plans for the summer togeth-er. I felt as though I had betrayed my beloved mother. I felt as though I had pierced her heart and as though my own heart was being pierced as well. I only wanted to give of myself this summer and learn all that I could. I didn't want to hurt anyone. For the first time, I felt like I might be doing something terribly wrong by going so far away to a frightful place and laying such a heavy, unbearable weight on Dad and Mom's shoulders. I didn't know how to console them and still go.

As I was preparing to leave, I could not reassure my parents that I would make it home safely. I did not dare make promises that were out of my control to keep. After all that I had heard about Calcutta — after all the dreadful depictions that had been painted so vividly in my mind — it seemed possible that I might return home to America in a black box.

On Friday, June 19, 1986, I left home for India. As I sat waiting for the plane to take off from Portland International Jetport, I looked out the window, searching for my parents. I could see Mom and Dad through the airport's big windows, wrapped in each other's arms, and I could tell that my mother was sobbing. I did not want to hurt anyone by making this trip. I just wanted to *help* people. The sight of my parents at that moment was enough to make me break into tears.

Three days later, I recalled this experience in my journal:

Sunday, June 22, 1986: *I hurriedly rushed through the Portland Jetport to catch my flight to Boston with hardly a minute to spare. Poor Mom and Dad were on my heels, blood pressure rising in all of us, hearts pumping — from racing to catch the plane, from fear about my leaving for India, from heartache and a terribly sad farewell. Kisses and hugs were quick but so very strong and meaningful. "Oh Mama, please don't cry," I muttered as our chins began to quiver. I had to run off so quickly and leave her there, crying. How could I cause so much heartache in my Mama? Thus far, this has most certainly been the toughest part about coming to Calcutta — leaving Mom and Dad with a terrible fear and sadness. I wish I could console them. I must return safe and sound to them, never to do something like this again.*

Mama, don't cry. It hurts so much to see you cry. I'm so sorry, Mama.

As the jet made its way down the runway, I could see Dad and Mom in the large, tinted window waving to me, not knowing if I could even see them. Mama was still crying. I began to cry. The plane sped by them and lifted me up into the sky. I began sobbing. . . .

Chapter Two

##

Having Faith Makes All the Difference

When you go out into the darkness, put your hand into the Hand of God, for that shall be for you better than light and safer than a known way.

AUTHOR UNKNOWN

Resting in the Palm of God's Hand

I had read that no traveler from the West could be fully prepared for his first encounter with India. I discovered that it was best to walk by faith toward this encounter — totally trusting God; this way is much more peaceful, and things work out far better when our hearts are peaceful and open.

My journey was long and arduous. It involved days of traveling, layovers in airports, sleepless nights, and unfamiliar places. As the airplane carried me across the Atlantic Ocean, however, I felt like I was being carried in the palm of God's Hand. I had a very clear sense of this. I felt like a child in that I was helpless in many ways — my life and safety were out of my hands to such a degree. I could not control whether the flight would be successful or not, nor could I orchestrate that the soon-approaching journey in Calcutta would be free from danger. I trusted simply that I would be taken care of, as the plane carried me across the world.

From Portland, Maine, I flew to Boston, New York, overseas to Paris, and to Bombay, India. Then I flew the most jittery, nerve-wracking flight of my life from Bombay to Calcutta. I appeared to be the only *non*-Indian on the entire airliner. I prayed during most of the flight. I was alone and uncomfortable, both in my seat (which was broken and would not recline at all) and in my feelings about personal safety on such a rickety-rackety flight. I was not looking forward to a rerun of this scene at the end of the summer — except that I would be on my way HOME then. What a tremendous feeling that would be!

Arriving safely in Calcutta, I counted my blessings once again. Wearing my rosary beads around my neck as Dad had encouraged me to do, I disembarked and headed with the other passengers toward the airport in the rain and dark of night. I had hoped that one of the Missionaries of Charity would be there waiting for me. They must not have received my letter stating my arrival date, for no one came to pick me up at the airport. I was completely on my own.

Arriving in Calcutta at such a late hour was the most difficult situation possible. My professor friend at Dartmouth had warned me that if I arrived in Calcutta in the middle of the night, I should *not* leave the airport and take a taxi alone in the dark. Instead, I should wait until daylight and then take one. Furthermore, he told me, I should sleep in the middle of the airport, under bright lights, instead of in a dark corner. I was grateful for his sage advice because my inclination would have been to go to a quiet corner and sleep!

God Sends Us Angels in Disguise

As I stood at the baggage carousel waiting to claim my luggage, an Indian gentleman came and stood beside me. He was approximately forty years old and fairly well-dressed. He struck up a conversation with me about an old, tattered book he was reading about JFK's death. He began to ask me questions, which I answered very curtly and with an air of disinterest in speaking. I kept remembering my Papa's words to me: "Don't be too trusting," and I tried my best not to be too talkative or friendly. However, this man continued to initiate conversation by asking why I had come to Calcutta. I continued to give *very* brief answers. Suddenly my luggage appeared on the carousel. I was saved! I gathered my bags, went immediately to the center of the airport, and settled down on a bench.

It was an eerie thing to see the faces of all the poor Indian people standing outside the big airport windows, looking in at the newcomers. They were just standing there, staring. Since it was so late at night, the airport started emptying out, except for a few others and me. So, this was it. I was supposed to sleep in the midst of these other long, thin bodies sprawled out on the floor of the airport. This was the last thing I wanted to do. I was eager to get settled into a safe little hotel room for a good night's sleep.

Within moments, the same gentleman with the book came along. Instead of just walking past me on his way out, he stopped and asked if I was waiting for someone. I told him that I was fine. He persisted with his questions, so I simply told him that I would be sleeping there until morning, when it was safer for me to take a taxi alone into the city. He could not bear to leave me alone like that. He stayed with me for hours, in the middle of the night, when he could have just gone straight home or to his hotel to get some sleep. He tried to make phone calls, to see if there was a room reserved for me at the YWCA. He bought hot coffee for me, and he stayed by my side.

When his efforts to make a simple phone call to the local YWCA failed miserably, this kind gentleman invited me to come with him into the city in his taxi. He explained to me that if there were no rooms available at the YWCA, then he would make sure that I had someplace to stay for the night. My first thought was that even the shadiest character might make an offer like that. I considered my options. Each one involved risk: I could either take my chances, go with him, and trust that he was an honest person who would truly take care of me, or I could remain alone there at the airport and try to make my way into the heart of this massive city alone the next day. I figured that at least with the first option, this man and the taxi driver did not know each other and therefore could not have conspired to hurt me. It would be safer to travel with the two of them than to travel alone with one male driver the next day. In spite of the fact that my Papa's words kept ringing in my ear, "Don't be too trusting!" I took a chance. I trusted that this man was truly a kind gentleman.

It was around midnight when we drove into the heart of Calcutta. There was no peaceful stillness in the night, not in this city. No one seemed to be sleeping. The streets were teeming with life. There were people all along the roadsides, fires burning, a great deal of commotion, and so many eyes staring in the windows of our taxi. There were dark silhouettes in motion everywhere.

Our taxi pulled up in front of the YWCA. Would there be a room available? The gentleman got out of the taxi, rang the bell, and waited.

I held my breath. It was the middle of the night, and if there were no rooms available, I didn't know what I would do next.

After what seemed like an eternity, a very tired-looking man came to the door, rubbing his sleepy eyes. The two men spoke a language I did not understand, but within moments, my gentleman friend turned to me with a smile and said that they had a room for me. My heart was bursting with *Alleluias!* Oh my God, thank You!

My friend continued to show his thoughtfulness by carrying my luggage into the entranceway of the hotel. He then bid me a warm farewell. I offered to cover the cost of the taxi ride, since it was the least I could do to say "thank you," but he refused to let me pay a single rupee. The taxi drove off and I never saw the man again. He is forever like an angel to me. I will always remember his mercy and I constantly thank God for bringing him into my life.[5]

As soon as I was safely in my room, I locked the door behind me, sat on the little bed, and breathed a huge sigh of thanksgiving. I made it! From the unfolding of events on just this first night in Calcutta, I knew that everything would be all right. I knew that I was in the best of hands. I could see that God was watching over me, and clearly taking very good care of me. I went to sleep with a smile on my face and my hands clasped in a fervent, thankful prayer.

When Mother Teresa first began ministering to the poor on the streets of Calcutta in her early days, she said: "At that moment I had the feeling that God had begun to bless the work and would never abandon me."[6] I felt the same comforting assurance, the same joyful hope, and the same serenity when I arrived safely in my little room in the heart of this city on the opposite side of the world from my home.

I prayed earnestly: "Please, dear God, protect me, keep me safe and free from all harm or illness. Please return me safely home to Mom and Dad at the end of the summer. Please ease their minds and let them know in their hearts that I will be home — healthy and happy — soon enough. And please, dear Lord, give me strength to do Your work, to love, to see beyond the frightening physical appearances of the poor and dying, to be attracted — not repulsed — by those in need with whom I will come in contact. Please help me to be strong and to do what I want to do. Help me to overcome any fears and inhibitions which would hinder me in serving. Dear God, please help me."

Letting Myself Be Guided

Lay all your cares about the future trustingly in God's Hands, and let yourself be guided by the Lord just like a little child.
SAINT EDITH STEIN

Early the next morning, I knew that I had to be brave and face the streets of Calcutta on my own, or else I might never do it. It was powerfully tempting to postpone it, and to stay secure in my room until I gained more courage, but I believed it was best not to hesitate. After a breakfast of little green bananas, hard-boiled eggs and toast, I asked for directions from people at the hotel. Wide-eyed and full of excitement, I stepped out onto the streets in search of Mother Teresa's convent. It was supposed to be about a twenty-minute walk, but I got lost. Standing amid the chaos of a noisy intersection, I wondered what to do. I truly stood out on the streets of Calcutta, a white-skinned female amid multitudes of dark-skinned Indian men. At first, this was very difficult for me. I did not want to attract attention and yet everyone seemed to be staring at me. I walked with my face down, looking at the pavement, trying in vain not to be noticed. Soon I discovered that being so conspicuous amid the multitudes was a real blessing in disguise. As I stood there feeling lost and confused, and apparently looking that way too, people started calling out to me "Mother Teresa! Mother Teresa!" and pointing the way to Mother Teresa's house! They seemed to know that a young American woman would not be in Calcutta unless she was looking for Mother Teresa.

God Guides Us All the Way

As to your way, God Who has guided you up to the present will guide you to the end.
SAINT FRANCIS DE SALES

I had never experienced *anything* like Calcutta. The streets were teeming with life, both day and night. There were cows roaming about aimlessly, interrupting the flow of traffic. Goats scurried along, weaving in and out of the vehicles and people. Men ran through the streets like human horses, pulling passengers in their rickshaws. Trams jingled and cars zigzagged around the trams and pedestrians. There were children everywhere, men buying and selling things, people staring, scratching, talking, coughing, and spitting. There was never a dull moment. It was an intense experience just to step out onto the streets of Calcutta.

I remember holding on for dear life to an Indian man who was holding onto the *outside* of an over-crowded, moving bus. I had my feet on the little step at the entrance of the bus, and if that man had let go of the bus, we both would have fallen off, onto the street!

I had never seen so many grotesquely maimed figures as I saw in Calcutta. People lay on the sidewalks, begging for rupees. One man, his face smeared into the ground, was so mangled that his gaunt legs were twisted horribly back up toward his head, where they shook spasmodically and kept hitting the sidewalk. I walked past one pitiful sight after another, and another. One old, unclean woman sat with a young armless boy across her lap. There were so many bodies with missing limbs — so many twisted, frightful figures.

There were black crows everywhere. They were like vultures. If you left your window open (because of the heat!) they would enter your room while you were away and scavenge through your belongings, tearing apart and clawing through anything that might contain food. They would claw through the piles of rancid garbage scattered through the streets, alongside the destitute people who would search for scraps of who-knows-what. The black crows, the dogs, the poor people, and the rats … all together.

Calcutta is one of the largest cities in the world. It is, by far, the most densely populated. It is a city where hundreds of thousands of people sleep on the streets at night. Where, out in the open on the pavement, thousands of people cook their meals, wash themselves, and conduct their daily lives. It is where they live and where they die. Sometimes as I walked to Mother Teresa's house early in the morning to attend daily Mass, I would have to walk in the gutters alongside the roads because the sidewalks were lined with the bodies of people who were still asleep on the pavement. At times, on my way to the different shelters throughout the city, I would reach down to touch a person lying face-down on the sidewalk, just to make sure he was alive, to make sure he was still breathing.

Like that first taxi ride into the city of Calcutta in the middle of the night, there was always a sea of faces everywhere. The air was dense with pollution and smoke, and the streets were filled with commotion, day and night. I am not sure which was more unnerving: the sight of this squalid city at night, or the sight of it in broad daylight.

Calcutta has been called "the city of dreadful night," the "Black Hole," and "one of the darkest places of our time." It is a place that is not easy to capture in words because one must smell it, taste it, step in it, feel it, see it, and listen to it to fully understand what it is like.

Calcutta must be seen to be believed. One does not know the meaning of the words "vile" or "putrid" until one has witnessed this city, teeming with life — the poverty, the congestion, the constant noise, the stench, the black dirt (or worse) that covers everything from the buildings to the people themselves; the big black crows, the beggars staring and tugging at one's sleeve, the sight of back-breaking human labor (people digging ditches, poor men carrying unsightly loads upon scrawny shoulders); the sight of stray dogs with balding, diseased coats ravaging through the garbage that lines the streets; the sight of animal carcasses hanging in the store fronts or being dragged along the roads in front of you as you walk. Everywhere there is a thick, black

I took this photograph from the window of a train to help explain to people back home how congested certain areas of Calcutta are and to try to give a sense of what I felt as I walked through Calcutta on my first day, alone.

grunge. Even nicer buildings are hidden behind rotten-looking exteriors and dilapidated walls. Along the roadsides, Indian men sit in the small, cluttered insides of their shops; outside, there is the incessant noise and activity. I often wondered what made these people move, and what gave them the courage and strength to haul, lift, and carry their heavy loads. What motivated them to get up off the dirty pavement in the morning and labor all day? (Actually, some did not bother to get up.) I saw so many people, many of them alone. The children hung around, cried, stared, washed themselves in the muddy-looking water at the side of the road, and scurried about. Although surrounded by multitudes of people, they appeared to be on their own. At first glance, everyone seemed so alone and unhappy. On the streets, hardly anyone smiled. After the dirt and the poverty, this is what I noticed.

My diary, Friday, July 4: *In the streets, men walk along carrying all sorts of bundles and things on their heads, from baskets to furniture to piles of bricks. It is amazing to see! They usually wear cloth wrapped up on top of their heads as a cushion. Other men push and heave long, wheeled platforms piled high with loaded sacks. Others pull rickshaws transporting passengers and goods through the city at a running pace. They run barefoot through these treacherous streets filled with rocks, holes, floodwater, mud and worse!*

In my first letter home, after getting more of a feel for the place, I tried to describe Calcutta, calling it a "struggling city." I wrote:

"I am still doing very well, staying strong and healthy, and keeping my spirits high…. Calcutta is like a black pit, a poverty-stricken, disease-filled, dirty, miserable place. The work makes it beautiful. And the people in the Home for the Dying, the mentally handicapped, the seriously ill, and the children (even in such disheartening, depressing conditions) sometimes possess such great joy and peace. It is unbelievable. With contentment and hope, some simply wait to die in peace with God. These people are inspiring and uplifting. I am happy and so thankful to be able to share in this and witness this personally. I find myself unaffected by the horrid environment and I am never depressed; I can walk through the worst slums (though not alone!) singing to myself and smiling inside. It is an awesome experience to find such joy in the midst of such ugliness.... I can feel your love and prayers each and every day. I can't thank you enough. It's like being with you and having you near. What a comfort!"

Mother Teresa once said: "We are able to go through the most terrible places fearlessly, because Jesus in us will never deceive us; Jesus in us is our love, our strength, our joy, and our compassion." God gives us everything we need. He is everything we need. By her life and words, Mother Teresa taught us to trust God. "Feel the security of divine providence," she said. "Trust Him. He knows. He will provide. Let Him test and trust our faith in Him. Wait on Him. Trust and believe."

It was a familiar sight to see groups of men around a pump or a broken pipe sticking out of the ground splashing water up onto their bodies, and washing themselves and their filthy clothing in the muddy-looking water. As I hurriedly made my way down the winding side streets to the Motherhouse each morning, I sometimes felt as though I were intruding into people's privacy — into someone's bathroom, kitchen, or bedroom. Everything in their lives was conducted out in the open air, in plain sight.

"The destitutes and the lepers represent the extremities of Calcutta's poverty. The norm is in a sense even more appalling for that is what this society appears to have settled for on behalf of the huge proportions of its people...." Geoffrey Moorhouse, *Calcutta*

Pictured: Rickshaw pullers are everywhere. They sit on their rickshaws and ring small bells to attract the attention of potential customers.

Before long, I was not afraid to be in a big city like Calcutta — even as a woman, even at times when I was alone. I felt safe on these streets once I became familiar with them. For the most part, the people I encountered in Calcutta were very friendly, gentle, and helpful, even amidst the worst chaos and squalor. I feel the need to explain what the outward appearance of this city was like in order to reveal my great joy in discovering the underlying beauty and greatness of Calcutta, and in order to put everything into perspective — both my experience and Mother Teresa's work among the Poorest of the Poor. This is the only way to highlight the endearing qualities underlying the appalling veneer.

As the weeks passed, I became part of the streets. The people along the roadways became familiar with me and I with them. I no longer lowered my head, trying not to be seen as I walked along, and the

"…at the bottom of the pile are those who squat upon its pavements, scarcely noticed in life by the people walking by…" Geoffrey Moorhouse, *Calcutta*. Pictured: Just down the street from Mother Teresa's convent two men huddle along the sidewalk on a rainy day.

people on the streets began to smile and speak to me more — although sometimes I did not understand a word that was said!

An Unforgettable Taste of Calcutta

A weird and marvelous and awful experience.
GEOFFREY MOORHOUSE, *CALCUTTA*

Indian food and I shared a mutual dislike of each other. I did not enjoy the taste of it and, by the way it seemed to behave inside of me, it did not care much for me either! Within my first few days in Calcutta, I had to take my first "medications" — two Pepto-Bismal tablets and one Intestopan (for stomach bugs, heaven forbid that I had any!). The latter was more of a preventive measure rather than a remedial one.

Some days, as we ate our meals, I felt as if we volunteers had stepped back into the Dark Ages. Sometimes we sat crossed-legged on bamboo mats for so long that the blood circulation to our feet was cut off.

Bowls of food were placed on the cement floor and doled out onto big, round metal dishes. There were no utensils. We ate everything with our hands — the rice, the eggs, the gooey dahl, everything. I tried to serve myself only the portions of rice, bread, dahl, jam, mango, etc., that had not been trod upon by the many bugs and other things which joined us. Often I had to fight off ants, flies, and crawling things through the entire meal. Eating became an unappetizing struggle.

Determining which restaurants were safe to eat at was all trial and error. If I got sick after eating at one place, I simply avoided it and tried another, one that did not make me feel ill. At one tiny restaurant, we ate the meal with our fingers from big green banana tree leaves covered with rice. The food was grim and it fit right in with the unsanitary atmosphere. I kept getting little rocks in my mouth and became more and more selective about which pieces of rice I picked up! I hesitated to look too closely at what I was eating. I regularly discovered that if I looked too closely, I would find all sorts of mysterious, unidentifiable (or worse yet, *identifiable!*) little black things in my dish — making the meal that much less enjoyable. Often, if I looked too carefully at my

There were people everywhere. Commotion everywhere. Noise, chaos, and offensive odors. Traffic honking and rickshaws weaving in and out of the hot, overcrowded streets, swarming with people.

food, I was certain that I could see what I had *thought* were spices running across my dish!

The sights were not always easy to bear, either. One day, at the Sealdah train station, two men passed by carrying a long bamboo stick over their shoulders. Strapped to the long pole between the bearers hung a human corpse wrapped up in plastic (in case it rained?), with the feet dangling out at the end of the package, swaying and bobbing up and down as it was carried along. This was not something you'd see back home in Maine!

My sense of smell was far too good. It made everything in Calcutta more difficult for me, as many of the scents of the city were far from pleasant. The source of these unpleasant smells was varied. Different areas often had their distinct stench. The neighborhood of the Prem Dan shelter smelled of the goat and cow skins that were hung over rails to dry in the sun, and this odor turned my stomach. The Kalighat shelter's odor was a mixture of human excrement, urine and decay; I wondered if sometimes the bodies in the morgue were beginning to reek. The corner of Freeschool Street and Ripon Road, which I passed by every day, had such a thick and potent stench that it almost knocked me to the ground. I tried to hold my breath as I passed by this area, which was used as a public urinal, but it did not help very much. Down the road a bit, when I had to catch my breath, I was bound to come across equally unbearable odors.

The tastes, sights, and smells were just a small part of the unexpected aspects of this experience. Everywhere I turned, there were surprises and inconveniences.

I Shared My Accommodations
with Many Living Creatures

Good night, sleep tight, don't let the bedbugs bite!

The place where I stayed throughout much of the summer had high ceilings, open breezeways, and young people from all over the world. There were also some features that I would *not* consider amenities, including the big black crows perched outside the open windows waiting to scavenge in the rooms for food. Worse yet, there were unsightly cockroaches the size of mice scurrying around inside the hotel. These cockroaches were about four inches long, and in the middle of the night, or in the darkness of early morning, they were everywhere! At night, as I lay under the mosquito netting on my bed, I could often hear creatures stirring in the room, getting into my bags, and rustling through my belongings. I did not dare to step out of my bed onto the floor.

Every morning I got up around 5 a.m. to get ready for Mass at the Motherhouse and to work in the shelters. It was pitch black outside at that hour of the morning. As soon as I turned on the lights in the bathroom, I was horrified to see the bathroom floor covered with enormous cockroaches. Most of them would scurry away as soon as the lights went on, but there were always a brave few that stubbornly resisted. This was so unnerving and disgusting to me. I would remind myself that I was not in Calcutta on vacation; I was there to serve the Poorest of the Poor, and this sort of thing went right along with the overall experience. If I had been in Calcutta on holiday, I would not have been able to bear it.

At night, the walls of the YWCA were decorated with long, translucent lizards. I had never seen such creatures before, and the sight of them sent shivers up and down my spine. Then someone told me that these lizards eat the bugs, and I began to think of them as my friends. Apart from the few unexpected "guests," the occasional power cuts, and the sweltering heat, the YWCA was a relatively clean and pleasant place to stay! Actually, I was very happy there and eventually grew accustomed to my surroundings.

Monsoon Season

. . . I was rushed out of the Home for the Dying around six o'clock, as the sky was turning fiercely black, warning us of a wild storm. . . .
MY DIARY, FRIDAY, JULY 11

Calcutta's monsoon season brings temperatures of 110 degrees and humidity of 100 percent. I had been forewarned that I would need to change my t-shirt three times a day because I would be drenched with sweat from the unimaginable heat and humidity in this city, and as predicted I perspired as I had never perspired before. During the monsoon, downpours burst unexpectedly and flood the streets of Calcutta in a flash. One minute I would be walking along dry, dusty roads, and the next thing I knew, I was walking knee-deep through a flooded city. It was a horrible feeling when the water rose to high levels — during the dry weather, I could avoid stepping in so many unpleasant things. I could walk far away from the places where people had urinated and defecated in the gutters; I could even steer clear of the puddles of spit everywhere. But once the floods came, everything was afloat. I had to walk through it all. It was a struggle, and I felt completely helpless. Most of the volunteers absolutely dreaded it when the floods came, but I embraced the floods. They helped me to understand just a little bit of the suffering that the poor had to endure. I would never have understood this part of their suffering if I had not been forced to experience it myself. And as horrible as it was, I still had it easier than those who lived on the streets. Eventually, I could make my way to "dry land" — to the orphanage, or to the

During monsoon season, torrential downpours flooded the streets in Calcutta. When the streets were flooded, people would steal the covers off the manholes (I do not know why) and you never knew, while walking through the flooded streets, whether you would suddenly disappear down into a manhole! It was necessary to reach one foot ahead and feel the ground to see if it was safe to take that next step.

Motherhouse, or back to my hotel. I could step up out of the flooded streets and find relief. But the poor had nowhere to go. They had to stay in it. Those streets were their only refuge.

Coming Face-to-Face with Beggary

Recall the face of the poorest and most helpless person you have seen, and ask yourself if the next step you contemplate is going to be of any use to that person.
MAHATMA GANDHI

The most challenging aspect of my sojourn in Calcutta was not adapting to the floods or tolerating the drinking water; rather, it was coming face-to-face with the most desperate human beings I had ever encountered in my life and trying to find meaningful ways to respond to God's children each day.

I had learned before going to India that nowhere in the world is there beggary on the scale found in Calcutta. I experienced this first-hand the entire time I was there. Practically every time I stepped outside my hotel there were beggars on the sidewalk to meet me. As I walked the streets, little children would walk alongside me, pulling at my sleeves and saying "No Mamma, no Papa — paise, paise!" (They were asking for "pennies.") On the rare occasion when I took a taxi, I was always startled by a hand suddenly thrust through the open window next to my face, and a pair of pleading eyes peering in at me.

Instead of ignoring the destitute people on the streets or walking past them, I tried to respond with some act of love,

Every day I came face-to-face with the most desperate human beings, and every day I tried to find meaningful ways to respond to these children of God.

Beggars were a fairly common sight. They ranged from women carrying children, to lepers missing limbs or fingers, to old men, to young boys and girls, to blind people. In this photo, a woman holds her cane in one hand and her metal dish outstretched in the other as she begs along the street leading to the Home for the Dying.

even if I could not remedy their situation. I would offer my food, when possible, or offer some rupees, or at least offer a smile. Sometimes I would reach down and touch the shoulder of a man lying on the sidewalk. I recall Mother Teresa's words that all we do is but a "drop in the ocean," but if we did not do it, the ocean would be one drop less and that drop would be missed.

One day, a man with no legs at all came bolting across the main thoroughfare and moved along beside me as I walked, catapulting himself along the ground with his long arms and the stump of his torso. He kept thrusting one of his arms up toward me, begging. If I had seen this on the streets of Portland, Maine, I would have been horrified. In this environment, this pathetic sight was not shocking or out of place. Calcutta, for the most part, was like a living nightmare. It was filled with human suffering and images that will always stay in my mind. What I saw was hard to forget. It penetrated my whole being.

An Attitude of Gratitude

There is no sweeter prayer on earth than a grateful heart.
FATHER ANTHONY DE MELLO

I was constantly giving thanks to God. His peace and comforting presence were with me at every moment. My eyes were opened to all the good things Our Lord bestows upon us every day at home in the West. I did not realize how fortunate we are until I was deprived of some of these blessings in Calcutta, and I saw so many people who were not able to enjoy any of the luxuries or even the basic necessities that we enjoy.

The water in Calcutta was contaminated to such a degree that I would like to have brought home a little jar of it to examine under a microscope to see exactly what was swimming around in it. I used water-purification tablets to kill off whatever microorganisms were there, but even so, I drank water that had particles of unidentifiable matter floating in it or that settled at the bottom of the glass. I kept recalling how, at home in the West, I could run water from faucets and drink as much fresh clean water as I wished. I could fill glass after glass with water without worrying about contamination or sickness. Without thinking twice about it, I cooked food, took baths, and watered the lawn with fresh, clean water. The supply of fresh water I had available

This is a typical meat shop in Calcutta, where the cuts of meat hang in the open air, exposed to the pollution from the streets, and baking in the hot sun. Flies hover all around. I always noticed that whenever the shopkeeper was not sitting there on the counter of his shop, whenever he went inside and was out of sight, huge black crows would come and perch on top of the meat, tear off chunks of it, and eat it. It is easy to understand why, temporarily, I became a vegetarian while in Calcutta. This whole experience triggered a response of profound gratitude for the quality of life we enjoy in the United States.

to me was seemingly endless, and yet I did not realize what I had until it was gone. Living in Calcutta's rock-bottom conditions gave me a new attitude of gratitude that will last a lifetime. I could never forget what I experienced — even if I tried. Even the bedbugs in Calcutta would make me grateful for a clean, comfortable bed at home. I would thank God every night before going to sleep! More than ever before, I understood: "How plentiful are the reasons for our gratitude to God! . . . Rejoice always, pray constantly, give thanks in all circumstances; for this is the will of God in Christ Jesus for you" (1Thes 5:16).

Calcutta seemed like one of the darkest places on the face of the earth. Yet, in this dark city, I would soon see "a great light" — and her name was Mother Teresa. As one volunteer put it, Mother Teresa reached out to the poor "as if it were God Himself lying there in the street, crying out for help." She changed an earthly hell into a bit of heaven for everybody, especially for those who were most in need of mercy.

Photo by Paul Hulewicz

Even if I learned nothing else in Calcutta but to appreciate everything we have, then it was well worth the trip. It has taught me to count my blessings, to take nothing for granted and to thank God for so many things, at least a million or two. In this picture, a little boy sits in an old pail on a Calcutta sidewalk. The pail may have been his bathtub . . . or his home.

Part II

Mother Teresa's Practical Lessons

Chapter Three

Our Mission in Life Is to Love and Serve

I have never found any true, deep inner happiness outside the context of love. Love (of God and others) and real inner joy have been inseparable for me. One does not exist without the other. Loving one another is what life is all about.
MY DIARY, JUNE 4

Putting Love into Living Action

Love turns work into rest.
SAINT TERESA OF ÁVILA

Mother Teresa always taught us to seek and find those who are suffering. She would say, "Find them, love them, put your love for them into living action." And that is what she always did. In Calcutta, I referred to the work we shared as "a work of love." Others called it "a work of grace," a "mystery of God." Mother Teresa always called it simply "God's work." It was God's love in action through us.

"Our work is to give service to the Poorest of the Poor," Mother Teresa had said. It is to serve according to the most basic human needs. Even though the work of serving the untouchables of society was difficult, austere, and even repulsive, Mother Teresa's missionaries seemed to do everything cheerfully, ardently, and with a feeling that it is a privilege to serve Jesus "in His distressing disguise." Their spirit of joy was contagious. This is one of the reasons why, although the work was physically exhausting, it was at the same time spiritually invigorating and uplifting.

I have always preferred working at "dirt-level," serving basic human needs directly — face-to-face, heart-to-heart, hand-in-hand. In Calcutta, everything was right there out in the open — the pain, the gratitude, the joy, the tears. Nothing was hidden. There were no barriers between us and those we served, only an honest sharing. This is what I loved. My time there affirmed that giving, sharing, and assisting others brings a tremendous sense of happiness and fulfillment.

Mother Teresa's Missionaries of Charity run leper colonies, AIDS facilities, schools, soup kitchens, homes for the destitute and dying, orphanages, and more all over the world. I visited and volunteered at several of Mother Teresa's shelters for the Poorest of the Poor during my first weeks in Calcutta, including homes for the mentally ill, for leprosy patients, and for abandoned children. I also visited food distribution centers, schools, and a shelter for the dying. The work ranged from changing babies' diapers, to tending lepers, to carefully removing the maggots from the wounds of a dying man. We were serving basic human needs, and Mother Teresa reminded us "no work is too lowly." Our job requirements, after all, included "a joyful willingness to do even the most humble work for the sick and dying."

No special training was necessary — the most important qualification was *love*. I learned that joy, laughter, a ready smile, and a peaceful heart brought comfort and eased pain. We received special graces to be able to do the work in the Home for the Dying. Without God's grace, we could not have done it with so much peace and joy.

After those first couple of weeks of visiting the various shelters throughout the city of Calcutta, I settled in at the two places where I felt that I could give my best and share the most: at "Shishu Bhavan," the home for abandoned and malnourished children, and at "Nirmal Hriday," the Home for Dying Destitutes. The intense, personal encounters in both of these homes were what brought such overwhelming *beauty* into an otherwise revolting environment.

The Children's Home

Let the children come to me, and do not hinder them; for to such belongs the kingdom of God.
LUKE 18:16

Mother Teresa's "Shishu Bhavan" is a home for all unwanted babies and needy children. This is the Children's Home where I worked each morning throughout the summer. The children ranged in age from premature newborns to approximately age eleven. And there were hundreds of them. They were fighting against a wide variety of infections — meningitis, dysentery, tuberculosis, malaria, and many other diseases. The babies had been rescued from dustbins, doorsteps, and railway stations; some were brought to the orphanage by parents who were too poor to bring them back to health. Others were brought to the Missionaries of Charity by the police, who obviously knew that Mother Teresa would accept them and take care of them. Some of the little ones were attempted, but failed, abortions. Fortunately, everyone knew that even if no one else in the world wanted them, Mother Teresa would welcome each one with love. "I have never refused a child," Mother Teresa said. "Never. Not one."

On my very first day in Calcutta, I was given directions to Mother Teresa's orphanage. It was located just down the street from the Motherhouse. I was told that I would recognize the place when I saw a long line of poor people waiting outside a big gate, for behind those big doors there was an open courtyard where food was distributed to the poor each day. The crowd parted for me when I arrived, and I went into the courtyard looking for the exact whereabouts of the orphanage.

After some wandering about, I went into one of the buildings and walked upstairs to a place filled with little children, and then into another room filled with even younger, tinier children and premature babies. So this was Shishu Bhavan! This was my new workplace. It was strange not to be given any instructions as to what I should do, even after explaining to some Indian women there (who did not speak English) that I was a volunteer and wanted to help. Without any guidance, I picked up a tiny baby who was crying and I comforted her. This is how I began working at the Children's Home in Calcutta. As the morning progressed, I tended to crying infants and toddlers: a little girl with the glazed-over eye which stared back into her eye socket was silently crying out for love and attention, and she seemed to keep losing her cloth diaper on purpose, hoping for attention and care; a child with purple-colored medicine on her lips cried for attention, too, and like the others, she enjoyed having her feet and legs and head massaged. All of the children seemed to be wearing little, checkered purple dresses and doing not much of anything. They stared at me as I held one of the infants. They watched me as if they were checking out the newcomer. They seemed almost too serious and meditative for their age. They were just sitting there, not moving.

The Orphans Were Hungry for Love

Give all to love; obey thy heart.
RALPH WALDO EMERSON

I was very surprised on this first day in the orphanage to discover a roomful of tiny toddlers sitting lifelessly on a cement floor. No one was playing; no one was laughing or talking. I was struck by how un-child-like these children were. It was as if their problems weighed too heavily on their minds. When that first tiny child began to cry and I took her into my arms, she IMMEDIATELY stopped crying. I thought: "Now *that* was easy!" When another child started crying, I thought the entire roomful of little ones would start crying at once.

I will never in my life forget the experience: as I tried to gently place the first little child back on the floor so that I could pick up the other little one who had begun to cry, the first child was clinging to me! Her arms were tight around my neck. It was as if she was afraid that once I placed her back on the floor, it might be a while before anyone came and held her again. I realized within five minutes of working in the orphanage that, more important than feeding the children or changing their diapers, more important than giving them medicine or bathing them, the *most* important thing I could do was to *love* them. I realized that these children had enough to eat, but they were hungry for *love*. Hungry for the human touch. During the course of the summer, I tried my best to love them. I fed them with as much joy and love as my heart could pour out. I held and cuddled as many as I could every day. I would hold one in my arms as I sat on the floor, rock another one on my knees, and sing to all the rest, trying to touch, in some way, all the children that I could; trying to make them smile and laugh all at the same time.

When I held the toddlers, they would often cling to me, and when set down on the floor again, they would either cry or silently stare up at me. All of the children were special to me, but there were a couple who truly melted my heart. One was my little "skeleton baby." She was a beautiful, brown-eyed girl with a swollen belly and fragile limbs. When

(Continued on page 62)

A TYPICAL MORNING FOR THE ORPHANS

Lunch time. Just before noon, all the children would sit cross-legged on the floor, on special mats, and we would spoon-feed the little dolls. The food was in small, metal bowls and it was usually something mushy. The tiniest ones were given a special baby formula with soybean. Mother Teresa described the formula as "first class — we have saved so many lives with it!"

Potty time. After lunch was over, it was "potty time!" Whether they had to go or not, we would take off their little diapers and set the children on their small toilets. Then we would stand back and wait for them. This was by far the most amusing and entertaining time of the day! The children were so adorable sitting on those seats, and they made me laugh a lot. Some of them did not even have to go, so they would rest their chins on their hands and wait for potty time to be over. Others delighted in using this time to socialize with all the others. Some would actually fall asleep and sink into their toilets, and we who were supervising would

This is a close-up of "potty time."

have to rescue them! One little girl seemed to think she was on a bumper car and she would slide her potty around on the floor and bump the other little children off their seats! There was never a dull moment during potty time. We really could not hold back our laughter and smiles.

Play time. "Play time" in the children's orphanage consisted of lively sing-alongs or teaching sessions where the little ones would learn their ABCs (in English), and time spent interacting with the volunteers. I never saw more than two or three volunteers in the orphanage at any given time. One volunteer, an Australian called "Auntie Ella," who was perhaps in her eighties and, like Mother Teresa, had enough love and enthusiasm to go around, taught the children many songs and loved them profusely. They, in turn, really came alive in her presence. If there were no volunteers around, the smallest children would be left sitting on the cement floor, staring at one another. I felt that there was not enough stimulation for the toddlers — so little to see, hear, do, or feel. Without sufficient human interaction, they remained silent and reflective. I also felt that they needed more love and affection. The Sisters and "mashees" (the Indian women who helped in this home daily) were wonderful, but more people were needed to provide the children with one-on-one attention and the steady stream of care and human contact children need. We volunteers did our best, but as Mother Teresa said, as much as we love the children, we cannot give what a mother and father can give. "It is impossible," she said. Nothing can compare with what a natural family life can give to a little boy or girl.

Naptime. After the children were all fed, their diapers were changed, and they had been given a chance to use the potty, it was naptime. We would lay the little children on cloths on the floor and set the tiniest babies in the cribs. As they dozed off to sleep, we would quietly slip out of the orphanage and onto the streets. I loved looking back over my shoulder at all the children sleeping. They always looked like little angels to me!

Naptime at Shishu Bhavan, the Children's Home in Calcutta.

(Continued from page 58)
I held her, she stopped crying, cuddled up to me, and rested. All that I could feel were her bones, all over. Her bloated stomach, rib cage, and her head made up most of her size. Her arms and legs were floppy, like thin dangling rubber bands; they were nothing more than skin-covered bones and her knees were the largest part of her legs. She was a beautiful child. So gentle-natured and sweet. I could not stop staring at her. Another child who totally won my heart was a precious little girl, "the quiet one." I would French-braid her hair, which felt so soothing to her that she would fall sound asleep sitting up! She was one of my *many* favorites. Maybe her big-eyed, silent stare attracted me to her. She was almost contemplative in nature, ponderous, knowing. She and so many of the other children were so motionless and silent.

The section of the orphanage where I volunteered most often was located on the second floor of the building. When I entered the courtyard of the orphanage and walked through the food-distribu-

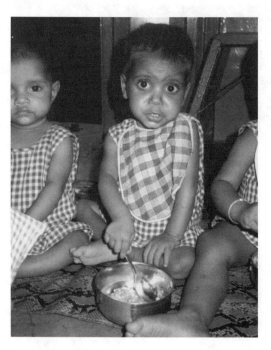

I used to refer to this little girl as "my skeleton baby." Her parents, who feared that this little one would die in their arms, had brought her in off the streets to Mother Teresa's Children's Home. She was severely malnourished and sick. Over the course of the weeks, she received medicine and nourishing food, and she filled out into a plump, healthy, beautiful, big-brown-eyed baby girl. It was so heartening to see a change like this. It filled my heart with hope.

tion area, I could look up at the second-story windows and see the faces of the children in the open windows. What a joy it was for me to see them! As the days and weeks passed, they grew very accustomed to seeing me arrive in the courtyard each day. In unison, they would call out to me "Auntie! Auntie! *Hello* Auntie! *Hello*!" Needless to say, this warm welcome from the upstairs window of the orphanage always brought a big smile

After climbing this final flight of stairs, I would walk through the Children's Home with little children clinging to both of my legs like fruit hanging on a vine. I loved being able to share my affection for these children. I could not have imagined how much joy and love I would receive during this experience.

to my face. I would return the greetings with a waving hand, adding, "I love you." I taught them how to say "I love you" making signs: first pointing to myself to say "I," then placing both hands over my heart to say "love," and then pointing at them to say "you!" I would send them this message with these signs and words and they would repeat it back to me, over and over, saying: "I-love-you!" I am not sure who was more delighted with this little ritual: them or me. I always felt like running all the way up the stairs to greet them, but I would walk, savoring each step of the way. When I reached the first landing, I was overjoyed to find a handful of little angels waiting at the top of the second landing — with huge smiles, bright eyes, warm hellos, and ready hugs.

Throughout the entire summer, my whole purpose was to LOVE! The simplicity of my life and purpose in Calcutta was a delight to me.

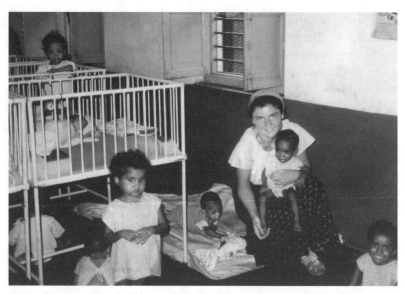

Even when I was tired, filthy, and so very hot, my heart was full of peace and pure joy when I was with the little ones. It was truly a labor of love.

From time to time, I must remind myself that even in America, my purpose remains this simple: to LOVE with all my heart and to put this love into living action.

"Each individual person has been created to love and to be loved," Mother Teresa taught us as we gathered around her, like children. Neither race nor religion matters, whether a Hindu, Muslim, Jew, Christian, atheist — "Every single child is a child of God — created in the image of God."

Finding Ways to Make Others Happy

Be kind and merciful. Let no one ever come to you without leaving better and happier. Be the living expression of God's kindness — kindness in your face, kindness in your eyes, kindness in your smile, kindness in your warm greeting.

MOTHER TERESA

It is true that the children in the orphanage were deprived of many things: families, freedom from poverty and disease, a carefree youth, even the out-of-doors. It was inspiring to join the volunteers in creatively finding ways to make up for the deprivation. For example, we tried to take the children outside as often as possible, safely and happily. We organized outings and took dozens of little ones to a big, open, grassy place where they could run and play and enjoy picnic lunches. One day, a small group of volunteers, along with some of the Sisters, took busloads of little boys and girls from the orphanage to the Calcutta Zoo! My Irish friend Paul, another volunteer, gave a little handicapped girl the best view of all by carrying her on his shoulders. I carried another little girl in my arms and she insisted on feeding the peanuts to me instead of the elephants! I laughed so much that day — the children were so playful and happy.

On Sundays, the volunteers made the long bus trip over the most congested bridge in the world to the slums of Howrah (the twin city of Calcutta) where the Missionaries of Charity Brothers work with the poor children. There we helped the Brothers take in literally hundreds of little street boys to bathe them, wash their clothes, cut their hair, and clip their nails. We did this outdoors in a huge open courtyard where there were dozens of faucets alongside a large building. It was always very noisy, chaotic, wet, and lots of fun! This was a weekly bath for these street boys, so there was always plenty of dirt to wash away.

I remember one particular Sunday morning, a hot sunny day in Howrah, I looked down to see a little boy looking up at me with big, brown eyes and an irresistibly sweet, silent appeal for help. I asked him if he had been bathed yet. That was a silly question. I smiled as I helped him to undress, found a big bar of soap, and washed his small body from head to toe. I lathered up his hair and scrubbed his little back, arms, and legs until we were both satisfied with the job I had done. Before I could begin bathing another child, he showed me that I was not finished with him yet — he quietly and adorably handed me his ragged, filthy shorts and shirt. Then he stood beside me as I knelt on the pavement scrubbing his clothes as best I could before hanging them on a line to dry.

When I finished washing his clothes, I had to go on to another child. As I sat on the ground with this new child in my arms, I looked

Several boys from the slums of Howrah cared for by the Missionaries of Charity Brothers.

over to see my little friend, this precious little boy, as naked as could be, huddled there beside me. He was following me. It was as if I had become his mother for the day. He, like so many of the other children, was not hungry for bread — but simply hungry to be loved, hungry to belong to someone. And I "fed" the children as best I could — with all my heart! I tried to let my little friend, and all of the other children, know that they were precious to me by the way I looked at them, the way I spoke to them, the way I cared for them.

Practicing Pure Love

There was an entire section of the orphanage filled with children who were mentally and physically handicapped. Blind, brain damaged, epileptic, disfigured. To love them was to put "pure love" into living action, one of my volunteer friends, Paul from Sweden, explained to me. It was easy and natural to love the more normal, healthy, and beautiful children, especially since they were so responsive to that love. We received so much in return for loving them. With many of the severely disabled children, however, there was no response, even when we sat for long periods beside their cribs and caressed their misshapen arms and legs. These children could not give us hugs and kisses. They could not laugh and smile. But how much they still needed to be loved! Some had constant spasms, some just stared off into space, some had eyes that were glazed-over or crossed, others were disfigured and simply difficult to look at. It was more pure giving and more pure loving to be with them. Mother Teresa would say: "We are all handicapped in one way or another.... Sometimes it can be seen on the outside; sometimes it is on the inside."

I spent some time in this special ward with the mentally retarded and physically handicapped. Many of the children were older, not infants. They were helpless and crippled, lying in their cribs. It seemed that they were left virtually alone. As I caressed the forehead and face of one young boy, I stared into his beautiful eyes. He was so young. He stared up at me so calmly and steadily, contentedly. It was a look of love and deep peace. He had nothing in the way of health, strength, or material things, and yet he seemed to *need* nothing except love. With the gentle touch of my hand and my fixed gaze, he seemed to be in heaven — he had everything. I listened carefully to his breathing, the breathing of a little child lying lifelessly in his crib. He was so young and innocent, suffering so much, yet at

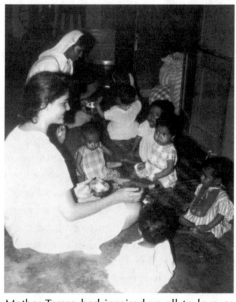

Mother Teresa had inspired us all to love as best we could. This was really what it was all about — filling the children's need for love and affection. That was my whole purpose for being there. In the words of one American writer, Mary Morris: "Love isn't something you wait for. It's something you do."

peace. When the work was difficult, Mother Teresa would think of those who were sick and suffering and she would tell God: "Look at my suffering children, and for their love bless this work." The response was always immediate, she said. These children were like the spiritual powerhouse of the Missionaries of Charity.

Many of the handicapped children didn't see much outside the walls of the orphanage. I sometimes thought the Home for the Dying was a bit easier to bear. I found more hope, more beauty, more peace within its walls. There, men and women rested during the last days of their lives — some of which had been quite full, others which had been filled with much suffering, hardship, and pain. A living hell. But whatever their lives had held, these people were nearing the end. No more worries, no more struggles. They were nearing an end and a new beginning. In their cases, there was hope for peace and new life. The tiny children, on the other hand, had a long way to go. I found it more difficult to see a child's heart void of the joy of life. They were so young and had their whole lives ahead of them. What did they have to look forward to? They seemed to have such a long and difficult road ahead of them — unless somehow they could be blessed with an end to their multifaceted deprivation. They needed others from outside the gray, dull walls to stimulate them, to bring sunshine, laughter, and love.

One day, I witnessed something very touching: I watched Mother Teresa as she was tending to two young mentally handicapped children at Shishu Bhavan. She was just shining on them — her touch and her smile brought so much peace, soothed so many hearts, and caused faces to brighten — even in the onlookers.

I saw for myself what happened to the children in the orphanage. The Sisters did their best to educate the children and to send them to school. Those who were healthy were put up for adoption. Those who were sick were given all the care the Sisters could give to make them well again. When the children grew up, they got jobs, got married, and hopefully lived normal, happy lives. If they were unable to live independent, normal lives, as is the case of those who were handicapped or mentally retarded, they remained in the care of the Missionaries throughout their earthly lives.

I made a second visit to Calcutta in 1991. During this visit, I was in a bookstore looking for a particular gift to share with a fellow volunteer.

There was a fine-looking young gentleman working there and he asked me why I was visiting Calcutta. As soon as I responded that I was volunteering with Mother Teresa, his face lit up and with a big smile he said, "That's my *mother!*" He had been one of the orphans at the Children's Home, and Mother Teresa and her missionaries had raised him. He was so proud and happy to be able to call Mother Teresa his mother. Of course he had every right to be! It pleased me so much to see how well he was doing in his adult life. Working in the orphanage for only a matter of months, I would not have a chance to see any of the little ones grow up or witness what came of their lives. I realize that this healthy, happy, handsome young man was only one child, one outcome, out of many; nevertheless, his success was a most pleasing discovery.

The "Little Terrorist"

Let us meet God with a smile — everywhere we go and in everyone.
MOTHER TERESA

There was one little boy at the Children's Home who was referred to as "the little terrorist," and understandably so. Occasionally, unpredictably, he would bare his teeth, open his eyes widely, and let out a shrill, unnerving laugh as if he were afflicted with insanity. Then he would attack whoever was in his path, biting and scratching and terrorizing his random victim. Even though he was only a little fellow, no more than seven or eight years old, he was a child everyone tended to avoid because his behavior was so unpredictable and wild. One day, while I was sitting on a bench painting the walls of the orphanage, I looked over my right shoulder and saw the "little terrorist" coming straight at me! The look on his face told me that he was ready to attack, and I immediately put down my paintbrush and tried to come up with a quick response. Only one came to mind: LOVE. As soon as he got within arm's reach, I took hold of the "little terrorist" and pressed him very close to my heart. He was suddenly disarmed, pacified, awestruck. He stared up at me with big, brown eyes as if to say that no one had ever done that to him before. No one had ever hugged him. He did not seem to know what a hug was, but he *liked* it!

From that day on, the "little terrorist's" behavior changed. The change was radical. He became a gentle-natured little boy. This young child approached me quietly and waited for a hug. He began to take time out from whatever he was doing, even from playing, to come and receive a kiss on the cheek and a big squeeze. It was so simple and did so much for him. In him, I discovered what a difference a daily, warm embrace could make in the life of a little child. I never saw him terrorize another victim. He truly seemed disarmed, having received what he did not even know he needed.

If only we could always counter the attacks of our enemies with LOVE! With love greater than fear.

"Our works of love are works of peace," Mother Teresa used to say. "Through our humble works we help our poor to recognize and recover the dignity that is theirs as children of God, created for greater things — to love and to be loved."[7] It amazed me to think that if Mother Teresa had not responded to God's call with a wholehearted "yes" and with living action, these shelters would not exist and this work would not be happening in

The faces of hope.

Calcutta and throughout the world in the way and to the extent that it is happening now. There is certainly much more to do and so many enormous problems to solve — truly this work is like "a drop in the ocean," as Mother herself had said so often — but at least she did *something*. She began a work of love that will not end soon, and she taught us in the most beautiful way, by her powerful example, how to begin — with "one, one, one" — one human being at a time, right where we are "at the level where we are called." If Mother had not answered God's call to give wholehearted, free service to the poor, literally thousands of people would have been left in the gutters to suffer and die, including the children and babies. When asked how she had accomplished so much, Mother so often responded: "Humanly speaking, it was not possible. It is God's work that has done it, not my work."

Bringing Joy from the Children to the Dying

Truly, I say to you, unless you turn and become like children, you will never enter the kingdom of heaven.
MATTHEW 18:3

As the summer months passed, I realized that it was a beautiful balance to work with the young children at the orphanage early in the day and with the dying destitutes in the afternoon. The children filled my heart with unspeakable happiness, and I could then carry this joy and love I received from the little ones to the patients in the Home for the Dying each afternoon. "How great is the humility of God to use people like you and me to bring His love and compassion to those who are suffering. Let us thank God for allowing us to be channels of His love," Mother Teresa shared with me.

I also had the opportunity to travel to a small village outside the city of Calcutta during my first couple of weeks in India. A lively volunteer from Australia, Moira, invited me. Moira was always making everyone laugh. Working with children was her specialty. She welcomed a small group of us volunteers to accompany her on this special journey to the countryside, to visit and entertain the poor people there. Moira taught us a variety of acts and mimes and songs. I personally cannot sing or dance well at all, but in that village, I sang and danced! I did whatever I could to bring joy to the people and lighten some of their suffering, without being too concerned or embarrassed about the quality of my performance.

First, we visited a leprosy rehabilitation center, where we entertained lepers and people who were mentally ill. As soon as we began to sing and do our skits, people from the village gathered outside the doors and windows to see us. One of the songs that Moira sang as a solo, in front of a roomful of people, was "Pretty, pretty Auntie Moira can kiss anyone better than you can," and she actually went around the room kissing people! It was a lighthearted diversion for everyone, including us, although it might have helped matters if the people in the audience understood English.

Our next "show" was for little ones. We gathered many of the village children together in one place and began to do sing-alongs and a whole assortment of things to brighten their day. After we finished our show, we asked if someone from the audience could come up and do some entertaining. I will never forget seeing three little girls come forward and do an Indian song and dance. Their voices were so sweet and their dancing was so beautiful! I loved the way they moved their wrists, hands, feet, and heads so gracefully. After they finished, I asked one of the little girls to teach me how to dance like that. Little did I know that this wonderful visit with the village children and this earnest effort to learn how to dance would make such a special difference in my experience back in Calcutta.

After I returned to the city, I resumed my work in the Home for the Dying. One afternoon, I was walking past the bed of one of the dying women in a dark corner of the shelter when I noticed that she was reaching up to me for some water. Her wrist turned in such a way as to remind me of the children dancing in the village. And so I began

Three little Indian girls dancing for children from their village and Mother Teresa's volunteers.

to dance. Although this frail woman had little or no strength left in her and she could barely even speak, as soon as she saw me dancing she began to laugh and laugh and laugh (I still do not know whether I should take that as a compliment or an insult, but it was obvious that my dancing really made her happy). It clearly brought joy to this poor woman to see Indian dancing — even at its worst! After that experience, whenever I walked past this particular patient's bed, she would reach up to me and turn her wrist, and I knew that it was no longer to ask for water — it was to make me dance.

I discovered that it did not take much to bring a bit of joy to someone, and whatever was given with a smile seemed to be accepted gratefully. I was often amazed at how brightly another person would light up from inside merely by being noticed, by being looked at or smiled at. During my stay in Calcutta, I wrote the following words to myself:

> Do not dwell in the darkness unless you can and will bring light into it. Do not carry with you negative thoughts or feelings unless you can transform them or channel them into positive and constructive thoughts, actions, energies. Be always a light to others, capable of dwelling in or passing through the darkest, most revolting places without adding to the misery, never dragged down in depression, never a burden to others.

Mother Teresa used to say: "We will never know just how much a simple smile can do." This was true everywhere I went in Calcutta, including the place where the poor were suffering their last agony — in Mother Teresa's shelter for dying destitutes.

The Home for the Dying

To a person who has slept in a gutter, the Home for Dying Destitutes must seem like a paradise.
AUTHOR UNKNOWN

The Home for the Dying has been called "Mother's first love." She believed so firmly that what the poor need is simply and above all *to be*

The rows of stretcher beds inside the men's section of the Missionaries of Charity's Home for the Dying Destitutes in Calcutta, India.

wanted. To Mother Teresa, they were all "children of God, for whom Christ died, and so deserving of all love." She seemed to have a place in her heart for each one of the poor, sick, and dying whom she encountered.

> Sometimes these people are taken from the streets on the threshold of death. There is scarcely anyone else in Calcutta who will even notice their dying. But the (Missionaries of Charity) have a refuge specifically for dying destitutes. It is right alongside Kali Temple.... It is a highly scrubbed and totally antiseptic shed crammed with stretcher beds, row after row of them, and their moribund occupants. There are people in their twenties, but hardly anyone looks less than sixty.... They have been brought here because of a ... conviction, unfathomable to the deepest dogmas of Hinduism, that there is some point in bringing a human being who has been totally neglected since birth to a place where he can at least die with a scrap of dignity and with somebody aware of his end.[8]

I volunteered every afternoon in the Home for the Dying. It is located in a section of Calcutta called Kalighat, which means "Kali's bank." Kali is the Hindu goddess of destruction, and Kali Temple, located directly alongside Mother Teresa's Home for the Dying, is an important Hindu shrine. The building, which presently serves as the Home for the Dying, formerly served as a place of rest for pilgrims who came to worship the goddess Kali. Sometimes, as we were caring for the patients in this shelter, we would hear religious processions passing by outside. Each procession brought with it a great deal of noise and commotion: ringing, chanting, and a corpse on its way to the burning ghats (an area where bodies were cremated) near the Hooghly River. It was bizarre to step outside the Home for the Dying, this place of peace, and to see these lively goings-on. Then again, it was a fitting experience for this city of contrasts.

Mother Teresa's Home for the Dying is called "Nirmal Hriday" in the native language, which means "Immaculate Heart." I refer to it as the "Place of the Pure Heart," and that is truly what it is. It is a place where love, in its purest form, is practiced every day. It is a place where hearts, through intense suffering and humiliation, have become very pure and holy.

It was a privilege to ride in the Missionaries of Charity's ambulance to and from the shelter for dying destitutes each day. This provided me with the opportunity to develop a closer relationship with the "Sister Superior" Sister Luke, the one in charge of daily operations

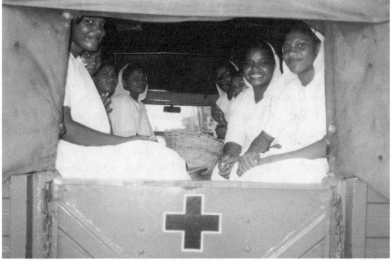

Every day, Sisters from the Home for the Dying go through the streets of Calcutta in an ambulance, searching for dying destitutes.

of the Home for the Dying. Sister Luke was a blessing and an inspiration to me. The ambulance ride also gave me a glimpse into the behind-the-scenes activities of the nuns. For instance, I learned that the Sisters always had their rosary beads within reach, and as they traveled across the city, they prayed. I also experienced their daily routine of picking up leftover food from a local business and bringing it to the shelter to feed the dying.

The street-dwellers were often able tell when someone on the pavement was about to die. They would flag down the ambulance when they saw it coming along with Mother Teresa's nuns. We would stop the ambulance, climb down from the back of it, and together we would lift the body of the dying person up off the sidewalk and carry him onto the ambulance. We would then transport this person to the Home for the Dying. There, we would give him a bath, clean garments, nourishing food, medicine, a bed, and a great deal of love. Without this shelter, many of these destitutes would simply die on the sidewalks, in the gutters, or in the alleyways, mostly unnoticed by the passersby.

Just Begin — One Person at a Time

Mother Teresa used to say that if she had not picked up that *first* person from the gutters, she never would have picked up the remaining 42,000. We all have to start somewhere.

The first day that I entered the Home for the Dying, I came upon the men's section with the skeletal remnants of human beings lying lifelessly in rows of stretcher beds. They were staring, scratching, and coughing. Many were silent. I felt as though I had been there before. It was just as I had seen in the black-and-white photographs by Mary Ellen Mark, and as I had read in various books. I stood in the middle of the main aisle, waiting for one of the Sisters to give me some guidance. I thought they would clearly see that I was a new volunteer and I did not know where or how to begin. I walked from the men's section into the women's section. I waited for a few minutes and then I realized that no one was going to *tell* me what to do, because they were all *showing* me what to do! So, I began to help them as best I could, by joining in the work and following their example. My very first task was to help one of the young Sisters lift an emaciated patient off her soiled bed, scrub the plastic bed covering with sudsy water, bathe the patient and give her clean, dry garments, and then gently lift her back onto her bed. We went down the aisle and helped one person at a time like this. One, one, one. My first reaction to the work was an exuberant inner rejoicing: "I can do it!"

Mother Teresa often used to say that what matters more than our actual deeds is the amount of love we put into them. The most important thing is not how many we help, but how we help each one. It was only in this perspective that we could say that what we were doing really mattered.

In Mother Teresa's Home for the Dying, one of the most difficult parts about being with the patients was that I could not be with all of them at once. As I was feeding a dying man, I could look up from his bed and see a dozen pair of eyes staring back at me, waiting to be touched and cared for. The same was true of working with the children in the orphanage. One must really take Mother Teresa's approach — that of loving one person at a time, wholly and fully. This is the only way to deal with all the suffering and work in a city like Calcutta.

One day in the Home I approached a man very near death who needed help. When I came to him, his clothes were stained: the smell was unbearable, and he was spitting up the most foul-looking matter.

In the men's section at the Home for the Dying.

His pelvic bone protruded more than anything I had ever seen before, even in the Home for the Dying. He was so skeletal. His cheekbones were sharp and pointed. His eyes were large, frightened, sunken, almost panicking. I had to change his garments and clean him. I hesitated, knowing how humiliating it must have been for him to be bathed and cleaned by a woman, especially in his condition. I found this so difficult. I had not worked much with the dying men yet. I felt they needed to maintain their sense of dignity no matter how small.

Given time, I overcame my difficulties while I performed my work. These words by Saint Francis De Sales became very meaningful to me: "Have patience with all things, but chiefly have patience with yourself. Do not lose courage ... every day begin the task anew."

We Are Channels of God's Love

Open your hearts to the love of God which He will give you —
not to keep, but to share.
MOTHER TERESA

Mother Teresa once said, "We started our work as the suffering of the people called us. God showed us what to do." I was clumsy when it came to cleaning up soiled garments and bathing the patients. I was better at feeding them and holding their hands. When the food was fully prepared, we would distribute it, hand-feeding those who were incapable of feeding themselves. After the meals had been eaten, it was time for washing all the dishes, distributing medicine, and simply loving. I told the patients how beautiful they were. When they tried to respond or smile, I told them I loved them and that I was happy to be there with them. Perhaps they did not understand my words, but they seemed always to understand what was in my heart. With Mother Teresa's Sisters, we volunteers would hand out water, blankets, biscuits, bedpans, anything needed. Some volunteers would assist in providing basic medical care if they were willing and able, like giving injections, dressing and cleaning sores, or setting up IV's. We would massage the arms, legs, and feet of the dying men and women, rub their shaven heads and protruding ribcages, listen to them and try better to understand Bengali and suffering.

Occasionally, I was asked to lift the body of a deceased patient from his bed. A white sheet was spread out on the floor, and we would wrap the body from head to foot, carry it to the morgue, and then lift the corpse onto a shelf. (I did not take the bodies to the nearby burning ghats as some of the other volunteers were called upon to do; I just took them to the morgue located inside the Home for the Dying). We would do whatever was needed most at the time — whatever was immediately in front of us. Above all else, we endeavored to keep our spirits high, and to carry a ready smile and a willingness to touch. I would do virtually anything that might bring joy and alleviate some of the suffering. As with the children, so much could be done for the dying. Sometimes having just a smile to give made a beautiful difference. As Mother Teresa said, "The miracle is not that we do this work, but that we are happy to do it."

Mother Teresa taught us that unless our work is "interwoven with love" it is not of much use. "God does not need our work. God sees only our love. He will not ask us how many books we have read, how many miracles we have worked, but He will ask us if we have done our best for the love of Him." (This is what my own mother always taught

My friend Bruce Aguilar, from the United States, sitting with one of the patients in the Home for the Dying.

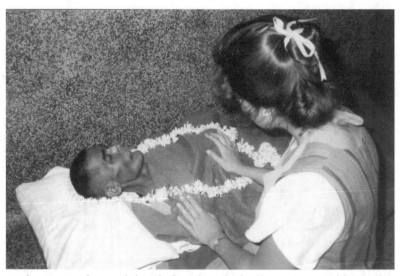

Mother Teresa dreamed that, before they died, all people would know that they were loved. In this photo I am saying good-bye to a man I had held until his last breath.

me to do, too.) Just using our hands was not good enough. We were called to also use our hearts and our whole beings. "Have we played well? Slept well? Eaten well? Nothing is small for God because He is almighty, and therefore each one of our actions done with and for and through Jesus Christ is a great success."

The work in Mother Teresa's Home for the Dying was simple, humble, and basic. It consisted of countless small deeds. It was just human beings helping other human beings. Giving cool water to the thirsty. Scrubbing the metal plates with ashes and coconut fibers. Cleaning and disinfecting the soiled garments and sheets in big open vats, and then carrying the laundry up to the roof where it would be hung to dry. Washing the floor on our hands and knees. Bathing patients who needed help. Carrying them to the small area where they were bathed. We were busy each day washing the patients' wounds, soothing their sores, but most importantly we comforted their hearts and prepared them for a peaceful death.

The patients grew accustomed to seeing my face each day. They knew that I was there to stay for a while. We became like family to one another — familiar and comfortable with one another. As the days turned into weeks, I learned what each person liked. Many found comfort in having someone to listen to them (even if that someone did not understand Bengali). One woman always wanted to have her skeletal limbs "exercised" by having me bend them and straighten them out repeatedly, while another patient enjoyed receiving a few extra biscuits. I knew that the fragile "skeleton lady" was not easily relieved of her suffering, but I could sit at her side each day, with her small hand in mine, and let her know that I wanted to be there with her.

Mother Teresa taught us in word and deed that what matters is the way we look at each person, the way we speak to them, the patient understanding and love we show to them with every encounter. There were some patients with whom I truly connected, and when they were taken from us, I truly missed their presence.

Through time, I also found ways to reach out to more people simultaneously. For instance, when I entered the men's section of the Home for the Dying, I would turn toward the patients, raise my pressed palms to my forehead in a traditional Indian gesture, and then greet the men with a smile and "Namaste!" which means "I bow to the light within you." I could, in this way, touch them all at once and watch their faces light up, one by one, up and down the rows of stretcher beds.

We had to overcome all our fear through prayer and love. Mother Teresa taught us in her writings: "…if you really love that person, then it will be easier for you to accept that person and [your service] will be with love and kindness."

"Love Proves Itself by Deeds"

All souls are capable of loving.
Saint Teresa of Ávila

"Many people *talk* about love and about God, but they maybe are not loving at all," Mother Teresa said to us. "Love cannot remain by itself — it has no meaning. Love has to be put into action and that action is service…. Our *work* is only the expression of the love we have for God. We have to pour our love onto someone, and the people are the means of expressing our love for God." These homes for the Poorest of the Poor were perfect places to experience how love and service are always related. Saint Teresa of Ávila said: "Love is always stirring and thinking about what it will do. It cannot contain itself."

In my first days at the Home for the Dying, it was clear to me that I was afraid to work in the men's section. Late at night, while I was lying on my bed at the YWCA, I could distance myself from Calcutta and reflect upon all the intense things that I had seen and experienced during the course of each day. I could also look at my own reactions. I realized that I had been avoiding the dying men; I had been going straight to the women's section. I was afraid. I had heard that the men die much faster than the women do. I was afraid to face death. I immediately resolved to overcome my fears and to begin working more with the men, starting that very next day. This made an extraordinary difference. I learned to work with love greater than fear. It was like opening a window to heaven.

"Love has no room for fear; rather, perfect love casts out all fear. . . . Love is not yet perfect in one who is afraid" (1 Jn 4:18). It was time to perfect my love.

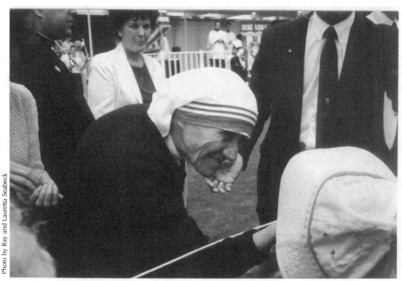

Photo by Ray and Lauretta Seabeck

In the book *Such a Vision of the Street,* Mother Teresa encouraged us to: "Love each other as God loves each one of you with a special, most intense love. Be kind to each other in your homes. Be kind to those who surround you." Here Mother reaches out to an admirer during a visit to the United States.

The Power of the Human Touch

LOVE and the gentle heart are but a single thing.
DANTE ALIGHIERI, ITALIAN POET

I began to spend most of my time in Nirmal Hriday, the Home for the Dying, with those who were closest to death. The more serious, critical cases were placed closest to the front of the ward where they could be watched over constantly. Every touch counted so much. Many of the patients whom I cared for and became close to, died. Sometimes the touch of my hand was the last human contact that a person felt during his or her earthly life. I learned to touch each person with as much love and care as possible. What a meaningful approach this was to each human being — to give my very best at each moment.

I found it much more difficult to face the multitudes of poor people on the streets in Calcutta than to face the dying destitutes in the shelter at Kalighat. On the streets I could only watch and witness the misery and aloneness and struggle; in the shelter at Kalighat I could touch and soothe the aching bodies and minds. Likewise, I understood how some of the journalists, authors, and tourists who simply passed through the Home for the Dying might have been terribly uncomfortable upon seeing the rows of suffering, dying bodies of the poor. What a difference it made to join the poor, to take a small part in their great suffering, and to try to lighten their burden just a bit!

One afternoon during my first week, I fed a woman with a large, foggy teardrop clinging to the edge of her eye. I sat with her, massaging her hands and face. She never uttered a cry or a word. She just watched me with those eyes. I went to the Home for the Dying the next day. I did not see the woman with the big teardrop, and I knew that she must have died. She most certainly could not have recovered. As I stood over her empty bed, Sister Luke reminded me simply that she was on her way home to God. I learned that time was very precious here in the Home for the Dying. Every moment was precious.

That day, as I rubbed the rigid, flesh-covered bones (no muscles) of another patient, I lifted my eyes and watched a small, skeletal woman shuffling along the cement floor between the rows of beds. She looked frail and death-like. I glanced around the room at all of the faces, at the very thin, brown arms and legs, at the sullen, staring eyes. Some people were crippled and had to be carried to the bathing area. Some could walk all by themselves. Others shuffled along, crouched down on the floor. Seeing these skeletal bodies creeping around the floor was like watching the land of the living dead. If I had seen this in a detached sort of way, without being part of the picture, I could almost have believed that I was on the set of a scary science fiction movie.

Sometimes I could do nothing for a patient except kneel by her side as she cried aloud; her body was in too much pain for me to even touch her. I could only soothe her with the knowledge that she was not alone in her agony. In order to avoid becoming disheartened or discouraged, I always had to be doing something, *anything*, to alleviate at least part of the suffering. Always, I was amazed at how the simple, human touch could bring such comfort to both the giver and receiver. It lessened fears and eased pain. I imagined that my hands were sources of light — light that emanated from my fingertips and soothed those whom I touched. It was really a beautiful thought. Our hands have so much to give, so much power to soothe aching bodies and souls, such comforting and penetrating warmth. Without the physical presence and contact, it was an unnerving, mortifying experience to be in the Home for the Dying. With it, it was an intensely meaningful and strengthening one.

My diary, July 2: "To tolerate the misery here, I find that I must be helping in some way to lighten some soul's burden. The human touch makes such a difference. The people dying in Kalighat are not frightening to see when you reach out and touch them. . . ."

"There are moments in the Home for the Dying when a visitor can believe that he has reached the backside of hell," one author wrote. Occasionally, visitors would come in and go on a tour through the shelter for dying destitutes. Sometimes I would watch them as they made their way slowly down the aisles, looking from side to side at the withered, wasted bodies, the shaven heads, the solemn, staring eyes. Some of these onlookers seemed to be quite uncomfortable, wanting only to turn on their heels and run out the door, slightly embarrassed by the awkward situation they had walked into — being sightseers in the Home for the Dying.

The overall picture can be overwhelming to see unless you yourself are immersed in it. The dying "bodies" ceased to be a frightening and repulsive sight once contact was made and a hand was held. That touch of a hand seemed to create a bond and to remind me that they were human beings, with hearts and souls and feelings — not just frightful-looking bodies. A friend of mine from Sweden, volunteering like myself, once asked me why I was not more afraid to caress the foreheads and cheekbones of these faces that were so gaunt and seemingly fragile. I knew that I was more afraid *not* to touch them.

Volunteers would sit with the dying patients, giving them everything possible, knowing them as brothers and sisters, and friends, caring for them with great care, respect, and tenderness, and occasionally sensing some sort of spiritual interference as an unexpected group of sightseers came on a tour of the shelter — sometimes busloads at a time — to look with pity on the lifeless "bodies." These tourists seemed to take away all that we had tried to give the patients. They stripped our patients of their dignity, by strolling through the Home as if it were a zoo. A certain measure of anger always swelled up inside of me whenever tourists came through. It seemed so demeaning to the patients. It broke my heart every time. I often felt that we had to start from scratch in alleviating the sadness and apparent humiliation of the suffering souls who were in our care.

In the film *Mother Teresa*, Mother said:

> God's love is infinite — full of tenderness, full of compassion. The way we touch people, the way we give to people, that love we have for one another — it is His love in action through us. Do small things with great love. It's not how much

we do — but how much love we put in the doing, and it is not how much we give — but how much love we put in the giving. To God nothing is small; the moment we have given it to God, it becomes infinite.

Doing great works *without love* is nothing, while doing small things of everyday life with *great love* is what life is all about. No matter where we are in the world, love brings hope, love gives comfort, love brings peace.

The work itself was not extraordinary; the Sisters and volunteers were just doing "the most humble work for the sick and dying," as Mother Teresa would say. Rather, it was the *spirit* of the work that was extraordinary: the spirit of love, joy, peace, patience, tenderness, and reverence with which each person was touched, held, and cared for.

There is a sign in the Home for the Dying with the words of Mother Teresa: "Let every action of mine be something beautiful for God." Mother Teresa did everything with love and care. The beauty of her love was that it was faithful and ongoing.

She taught us to "pray the work." And indeed every touch, every glance, every word was a prayer.

Love and Joy Are Understood Everywhere We Go

Miriam was one of the patients in the Home for the Dying to whom I became especially close. One reason for our closeness was that, throughout the entire summer that I was in Calcutta, she lived. Most of the other patients had not survived, so I never had a chance to become friends with them. Also, Miriam had a wonderful, feisty spirit that charmed my heart. Whenever I sat on the side of her bed, she would swing her arm up over my lap. She let me rub her feet. I quickly learned that Miriam loved the special high-protein biscuits, and from time to time she would say to me "biscoooot!" and I would go into the cupboards to get some extra biscuits for my friend.

Amazingly, I encountered no language barrier while I was working with the poor and dying people of Calcutta. The fact that I did not know how to speak Hindi or Bengali, except for a few important phrases like "hello" and "I love you," was not a problem in the least. I learned that

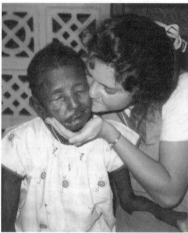

Miriam was precious to me. Even though she was on the verge of death, with so little life remaining within her tiny body, she would hold me around the neck as I sat on the edge of her bed. She would pull me near and hug me. It made me so happy just to sit at her side, watching her every move, no matter how slight, holding her cold hands, and rubbing her shaven head. Miriam had tuberculosis.

listening is often more important than speaking when it comes to comforting those who are in pain. I learned that love truly is a universal language that is understood everywhere it is spoken.

I was able to tell Miriam everything I wanted her to know — simply through feeding her, holding her, rubbing her back, and making her smile. She, in turn, showed me her love, gave me her hand and accepted what little I had to offer. "When we speak the language of God's love, the barriers drop and everyone understands," one Sister said. And this is what I experienced.

Trusting in God "With the Simple Faith of a Child"

Miriam was about forty years old and dying of severe tuberculosis. I remember being told by one of the other volunteers that whenever I was holding someone with this disease, I should follow this litany of precautions: as soon as they began to cough that deep tuberculosis cough, I should set them down, pull away from them, turn my head, hold my breath, and wait as long as I could before returning to them. This all sounded fine and good, but in reality, it was not practicable for me. One day, when Miriam seemed to be close to dying, I was holding her and trying to comfort her. When she began to cough, the last thing I wanted to do was to let go of her or turn away. This was true with all the patients. I prayed in my heart: "Dear God, if I forget myself in order to take care of this person in my arms, will You please take care of me?" He always responded beautifully to my request.

I never came down with any of the diseases or strange illnesses to which I was constantly exposed. I remember that, at one point, there was a problem with "red-eye" spreading like wildfire throughout the Home for the Dying: the patients, volunteers, and even the Sisters were contracting it. Although it was highly contagious and an unnerving sight, I remained free and clear of it. One of my volunteer friends returned home to England with amoebic dysentery; by the time she was cured of it, she came down with tapeworm. Another young woman was trying to make her way home to Canada, and she had to spend three weeks in a hospital in Dublin with hepatitis. An American volunteer friend of mine went home with lice and scabies and could not rid herself of them for about six months. These were some of the risks we faced as volunteers.

I attribute my personal well-being in Calcutta to two simple things: 1) God's mercy in response to my prayers for His protection. Our Lord said, "Ask and you shall receive" (Mt 7:8), and He was very kind to me when I asked Him "with the simple faith of a child" to watch over me as I watched over the poor and dying. 2) My joy at being there doing what I was doing. If I had allowed myself to become depressed or discouraged, I believe that I would have been much more susceptible to all the different germs and diseases. As Mother Teresa said so beautifully, "joy is strength." Faith and happiness were my greatest preventive medicines while I was in Calcutta. God's grace and God's will maintained my health.

We Are Called to Be Faithful

Some people who visit the Home for the Dying naturally are upset about the way this place is run, the quality of medical attention, and the overall conditions. I was not at issue with the goings-on, because I was more attuned to the spiritual side of what was happening there — the love, the peace, the joy, the tenderness with which the patients were cared for — more than the medical side, which was not the least bit "high tech," but neither was it meant to be. As Mother Teresa has said in the past, "God has not called me to be successful; He has called me to be faithful." To me, it was a beautiful place, a place where people died in peace with God after being loved and cared for like angels. "I don't want the work to become a business, but to remain a work of love," Mother Teresa said. And that is what her work was and continues to be.

Mother Teresa was once asked: "Why do you give them fish to eat? Why don't you give them a rod to catch the fish?" She responded: "But my people can't even stand. They're sick, crippled, demented. When I have given them fish to eat and they can stand, I'll turn them over and you give them the rod to catch the fish!"[9] She felt that we each have a role to play in serving those in need. She understood that there are many different levels of service, each of them important. Mother Teresa personally was called to serve at the level where people could not even help themselves; she was called to do work that was essential, and to do work that most of us would never care to do.

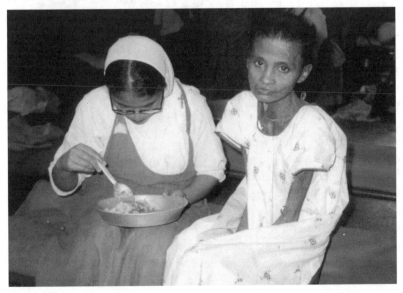

A young novice of Mother Teresa's missionaries feeding a patient in the women's section of the Home for the Dying. Serving in this shelter is an important part of their training. It is like taking classes in the best school of love.

"Peace to All Who Enter"

Let us always meet each other with a smile ... for a smile is the beginning of love.

MOTHER TERESA

The Home for the Dying is a place where the poor die within sight of someone who cares. Mother Teresa said: "We help them all die in peace with God. I don't think anyone here has died without making peace with God." Even though the patients were often coughing and spitting, and some of them had open wounds and sores, and the work was unappealing to most people, at first the newness of the experience made it easy to go to work each day. After a while, however, the newness began to wear off a bit. Then it became more challenging to be faithful to the work and to keep going back.

At the entrance to the Home for the Dying: "Peace to all who enter."

I knew, though never precisely, what to expect each day in the Home for the Dying. One of the difficult aspects was the stench, which at times was unbearable. The strong odor of disinfectant, human waste, and death all blended together and offended my all-too-sensitive sense of smell. Right inside the entrance of the Home for the Dying there was a small wooden cross that read: "Peace to all who enter." Many times I would pause at that cross, touch it, and brace myself before going inside.

As I entered, I would remind myself why I was there and what I hoped to do. That helped to give me courage. After saying a prayer to

God, the Great Healer, I would pass through the men's section and greet them all at once and watch so many faces brighten up, like a string of lights.

Although I grew accustomed to the workings of the Home for the Dying, there was still much to learn. One day, I gave an injection to a woman who was suspected of having leprosy. She had gaping holes in her face, holes that went straight through to her jawbone, teeth, and skull. I had never served anyone with such a frightful appearance, and I had never before in my life given anyone an injection. With a little training, I did it.

Some of the injections were intended to be intra-muscular injections — but we could not find any muscle at all in many of the patients' limbs. It was pitiful to watch these injections being administered, because there was nothing but skin-covered bone. The thought alone made me wince. We really needed to keep our courage as we kept trying to serve in any way we could. While doing so, we were experiencing one of the great lessons of Saint Francis of Assisi: we received so much while giving of ourselves.

I'm standing in the street in front of the entrance to Mother Teresa's Home for the Dying in Calcutta. The Home is next door to Kali Temple, a shrine dedicated to the Hindu goddess of destruction.

"It Is in Giving that We Receive"

When you let me take, I'm grateful.
When you let me give, I'm blessed.
AUTHOR UNKNOWN

It was not easy to say who was receiving more during the afternoons I spent in the Home for the Dying.

The Sisters and volunteers who were medically trained would put tubes through the nostrils down to the stomachs of some patients who could no longer take in any solid food, so that they could at least receive nourishing fluids. One day this arrangement was not working well for a man who was dying of tuberculosis. This man kept vomiting in his bed and losing all the nourishment that they were trying to give him. A couple of nurses from England called out and asked if there was anyone who would volunteer to sit on his bed and hold this man in an upright position so that the fluids would drain down into his stomach and hopefully not be lost. My hand went up immediately. How I wanted to help in this way! All summer long, I had been able to sit at the patients' bedsides taking care of them, feeding them, holding their hands, but this was a chance to really *hold* someone. I sat on his bed and the nurses propped his body up against mine in a sitting position, and all afternoon I held him. I will never forget that experience, or how he looked up at me the whole time that I cared for him. I was deeply touched by his silent stare, his large innocent eyes, his young face, and the way that he gently caressed my hand as I held him. Who was comforting whom, I wondered? Who was giving more joy, peace, and strength to whom? Until the time of his death, he gave me everything he had to give.

I thought that I would go to Calcutta and bring joy and relief to those who were suffering, but I never imagined that they would love and comfort me in return. I simply was not expecting this, and it touched me deeply. In silence, I remained with this man for hours, just holding him as he caressed my hand. We took care of each other. My young friend died during that same night, yet not until he had given everything, every bit of love he had left to give. It was almost as if he was somehow fulfilled and his life was somehow made complete that afternoon. I felt the same way about my own life. My heart and soul were so full.

One might think that these dying patients had nothing left to give, that they could only receive love and comfort and tenderness; but this was not so. This young man proved that he could offer love all the way to his last breath. After he died, Sister Luke told me that we were the same age — we were both twenty-one.

Sometimes I Failed to "Love Until It Hurts"

Love to be real must cost; it must hurt;
it must empty us of self.
MOTHER TERESA

One time I left the Home for the Dying late in the evening. I walked through the Home in the dark. All of the volunteers and Sisters had gone. It was just the dying people and me. As I walked along the aisles, I looked at their faces and reached out to touch their feet as I passed the foot of each of their beds. I was surprised to see they were not sleeping. They were awake and alert in the silence, stillness, and darkness of evening, as if they were waiting for the night to pass. My heart was moved with pity. One woman reached up to me with trembling arms. I could not resist stopping and staying with her for a while. This was one of my saddest memories because it is one of the few deep regrets I have. She was soiled from head to toe. Her bed was a mess. She smelled badly. I held her hands and spoke with her softly. We smiled a lot at each other. But in the dark, I did not know how I could carry her into the bathing area alone. I had never carried or bathed anyone all by myself. There were no windows there, no light. I did not know if I could even find the soap in the dark. Furthermore, it was so late that I knew it would be a little dangerous for me to be traveling through the city at night alone. I thought it would be wisest if I got started on my journey soon. After my visit with this woman in the dimly-lighted Home for the Dying, I got up and waved to her as I parted. I always remember this experience. I wish so much that I could have done more for her that evening. I felt that I failed to "love until it hurt."

Helping People to Die "Like an Angel" with Love

Speak tenderly to them. Let there be kindness in your face,
your eyes, in your smile, in the warmth of your greeting.
Always have a cheerful smile. Don't only give your care, but
give your heart as well.

MOTHER TERESA

Mother Teresa invited people to "come to our Home for the Dying to smile at them, to be with them." It was good for us to remember that death is not the end of life, it is merely a change in life, and dying people are living people in need of love and care. They are just like us.

Longing to learn, we volunteers came face-to-face with the great mysteries of life, love, suffering, and death. I felt that we were discovering, in the harsh reality of Calcutta, the basic ingredients of a happy and fulfilling life. These ingredients had very little to do with money, power, or prestige. They have much to do with love, sharing, and an intense spiritual life. Having been in constant contact with the dying in Calcutta, I could not help but ponder the inevitability of death.

Mother Teresa taught us in her writings: "People are afraid of what will come, so they do not want to die. If we do [know what is to come], if there is no mystery, we will not be afraid. There is also the question of conscience — 'I could have done better.' Very often as we live, so we die. Death is nothing but a continuation of life, the completion of life. The surrendering of the human body. But the heart and the soul live forever. They do not die. Every religion has an eternity, another life; this life is not the end; people who believe it is, fear death. If it was properly explained that death was nothing but going home to God, then there would be no fear."[10]

Mother Teresa used to say that giving happiness and relief to one person is worth taking the trouble. "I remember one of the first men we brought here," she said. "I found him lying in an open drain. He was in terrible condition. After we cleaned him and put him to bed, he told me: 'All my life I've lived like an animal on the street, but here I'm going to die like an angel, loved and cared for.' He died three hours later with a peaceful smile on his face."[11]

The patients whom I personally held and cared for in the Home for the Dying did not speak words of gratitude like this man did to Mother Teresa, but their faces, their expressions, their grateful smiles said as much as any words ever could. I was profoundly moved by the appreciation I saw in their faces. I was amazed at the spirit of surrender in many of these patients. Although some of them cried aloud, many of them had quietly surrendered to all that was taking place in their lives.

I recall one incident where I had given one man, whom I called "Sir," special attention for two days as he neared his death. I sat on his bed against the entrance wall with his body propped up against mine. He kept staring up at me, with his teeth bared as if he were smiling incessantly. On the second day as I sat with him, the man in the next bed was found to be dead. As I watched the dead man's body being taken to the morgue on a metal stretcher, I looked back down at my dying man, "Sir," knowing that his turn would soon come. It made my heart ache to look around the room at all of the men staring sadly at the goings-on. They knew exactly what was happening and where they were. No one uttered a cry. I honestly didn't understand why not one soul cried.

One of the toughest parts about working with the dying was coming in to work and seeing an empty bed where I had cared for a special patient during previous days. This filled me with a sense of sadness and loss, and I felt the need to stop and pray. Mother Teresa had said: "This is the greatest gift God has given you: having the strength to accept anything He might give you and be willing to give back to Him anything He might ask of you."

Yet, there was something very beautiful, consoling, and hopeful about death in Nirmal Hriday. The men and women there had been brought in off the streets. Most of them had lived lives of suffering, hardship, and pain in that "hell on earth." In this shelter, the patients were nearing the end of their lives — not unnoticed, but *loved*, not lying in a gutter, but lying in beds. Many of the patients still suffered greatly — whether they were filled up with cancer or enduring the effects of dysentery or struggling to breathe with severe tuberculosis. They were nearing the end of their suffering — a time when everything would somehow be made right, a time when they had hope for *peace*.

"Don't Be Afraid; I'm Right Here With You"

Mother Teresa's hope was for each person to die in peace and with dignity, with someone aware of their end. She wanted someone to be with each person as he took his last breath, so that when he left this world, he was surrounded with love.

Sometimes I did not even know the patient's name as I held him; but there was comforting familiarity between us and at certain moments a deep communion of souls. I would sit for hours at a time at a bedside, caring for a patient as best I could, and we would look at each other, stare into each other's eyes. Only with love can we restore human dignity. Only with love can we bring peace.

By far, the most difficult part about the death in the Home for the Dying was that so many patients seemed to die alone in their beds in the middle of the night. I had a silent but very fervent prayer in my heart that someone, anyone, could be there with them, holding their hands, comforting them and saying, "It's all right, don't be afraid, I'm right here with you...." Even if the poor soul did not understand En-

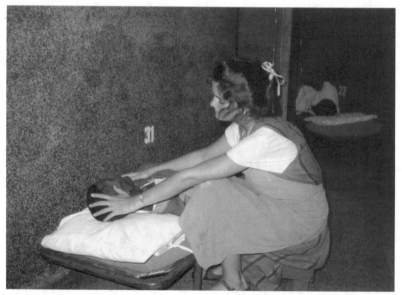

I felt that the only *lasting* impressions we made in the Home for the Dying were spiritual and invisible — we left our fingerprints on the souls of those whom we had loved and served.

glish, he would understand that someone was with him and that someone cared. Death doesn't have to be frightful thing to face. With love
and companionship, so much of that fear goes away. I would see this
prayer of mine answered — at the end of the summer when I watched
a man die in a volunteer's arms. I just happened to be the volunteer.

It is not with the noise of words, but with the longing of our hearts
that God hears us, Saint Teresa of Ávila said. God heard my unspoken
prayer that these dying men and women would have loving companionship during their last moments. He answered it in a way that made me cry.

When I arrived at Kalighat that morning, I discovered that my
most dear, gentle, smiling man whom I had loved so much, "Sir," had
passed away. I knelt at the entrance of the morgue and prayed for his
soul. Each word I prayed on this man's behalf went directly to God,
purely and immediately. More than ever before in my entire life, I felt
as though I could reach out and *touch* God. It was as if He was right in
front of me. I was speaking to God, so simply, directly, and clearly. I
could feel that Our Lord was shining upon me lovingly.

Then, I sat with an unfamiliar dying man, a new arrival. Everyone
was preparing for Holy Mass, which was going to be celebrated right
there in the men's section of the Home for the Dying. This special day
came on the Feast of the Queenship of Mary, August 22. This date had
added significance for it was also the anniversary of when Mother Teresa first opened the Home for the Dying in Calcutta. This was the very
first of all her homes for the destitute and dying. There were leis of
flowers, singing, and a great deal of excitement in the air.

There was heavenly singing in the background as I sat at the dying
man's side, wrapped up in my own little world. The Sisters were re-
hearsing their hymns. The newcomer was breathing heavily and with
terrible difficulty. His eyes stared upward in the direction of a statue of
Our Blessed Mother. His mouth was covered with cuts and sores; his
lips were disfigured and misshapen. A few uneven teeth were protruding from his mouth. As I held his head and caressed his brow he died
… so gently, so naturally, so peacefully, with his head and hand in my
own hands. He did not die alone and frightened but with someone —
someone who noticed his death and cared.

Just as I noticed his gentle death, I looked up to see Mother Teresa
herself entering the room within an arm's reach of me. I reached out to

her and she took my hand. I whispered something to her about this man having just gone to God and about how I felt deeply privileged to have been there with him during this gentle transition. I was deeply moved by the realization that I was holding and loving this man when he died. I felt so grateful. Mother Teresa helped me to close his eyes and fold his hands, blessing him. This was the special answer to my inner hope. I've never felt so cared for by loved ones above. It felt like a blanket of peace had been laid over us by God.

As I was whispering my gratitude to Mother Teresa for this special privilege of being with this man at such a sacred moment, I began to cry. It was not out of fear, but out of being deeply touched by this experience. She looked directly into my eyes and said: "You have received many graces for this." I did not understand exactly what she meant by this, for I felt that I owed God thanksgiving and praise for the honor of being with this poor man. God did not owe *me* anything.

After saying a prayer for the man I had held, I watched Mother Teresa with the dying patients in the women's ward. Then I approached her and Sister Luke as they stood there. I burst into tears when I tried to express to them what a true privilege it had been just minutes before to have had that beautiful experience. They both understood, though everyone around us — Sisters, volunteers, mashees — wondered why I was so terribly distraught and saddened. They didn't know that mine were tears of gratitude.

Since I had been prepared to encounter a hell on earth, I was not overwhelmed when I came face-to-face with the poverty, suffering, disease, and death I found in Calcutta. I was expecting these things. But I was brought to tears by the incredible beauty I found amidst the ugliness of this city, the joy amidst the terrible suffering, the peace amidst the noise and confusion, and the life amidst the constant death. In this "hell on earth" I really experienced heaven.

Mother Teresa Reached Out to All People with Love

One of my favorite things about Mother Teresa was that she treated each person with the same respect and indescribable kindness. She interacted with a dying destitute in the gutter in exactly the same attentive way that she interacted with a president, a pope, or a princess.

Those who had absolutely nothing were treated the same way as those who had it all. This was extraordinary to me. Everyone felt loved in her presence. She had a way of making each person feel special.

Although she was world-famous, Mother Teresa did not pull away from ordinary people. Rather, she continued to let the little ones keep coming to her, keep touching her, and keep being touched by her. She let them speak to her, listen to her, and be near her. She was very approachable and generous with her time and love. She did not reserve her energy and attention just for "important" people, and she certainly did not keep it for herself. After evening prayer, for example, the Sisters would leave the chapel and begin preparing their evening meal. Mother Teresa would stay behind in the chapel, with us. She used to pull a little wicker stool into the center of the wide-open chapel floor and we would gather around her feet, asking her questions, and listening attentively to her answers. With great love and simplicity, she would speak to us about anything we wished. Poverty, human suffering, wealth, prayer, God — we were unspeakably happy on these occasions! We felt so blessed! Her words were profound, yet they had the simplicity of truth. Even a child could understand them.

I noticed that unless one of us from the group spoke up and dispersed the gathering so that Mother Teresa could go and have her evening meal, Mother herself would never think of leaving us. She never seemed

The most beautiful thing was to see how Mother Teresa interacted with people. She looked upon each soul as if it had no equal, as God does. "I believe in person-to-person," she said. "Every person is Christ for me, and since there is only one Jesus, that person is the only one person in the world for me at that moment."

Photo provided by the Missionaries of Charity

to think of herself. She was always giving, giving, giving, without counting the cost to herself.

My mother had been diagnosed with cancer during the autumn before my journey to Calcutta. She had endured so much suffering and the prognosis was not hopeful in the least. I remember sitting alone with Mother Teresa one day and asking for her special prayers for my mother at home. The look on her face was so compassionate. She told me that she would pray for my mother — and then she excused herself and disappeared behind a curtain. After a few moments, she reappeared and placed into my hand a precious gift: two beautiful Miraculous Medals. One for me and one for my mother. She told me that I should wear my medal close to my heart, and I did so immediately, just as soon as I could find a little piece of string to tie the medal around my neck. When the summer was over, I carried the second Miraculous Medal home to my mother, with great love and joy. My mother is still with us, and anyone who knows her will understand that I could never be grateful enough for this priceless blessing!

Years later, my younger sister, Ruthie, was suffering through the unexpected and sudden breakup of her marriage. With tears streaming down my face, I wrote to Mother Teresa begging for her prayers. I was heartbroken by what was happening. Mother Teresa responded with two beautiful letters — one for me and one for Ruthie.

Mother Teresa's thoughtfulness made both of us cry. She had people dying in the gutters in Calcutta, and yet she took the time to write a personal letter to each of us, consoling us and encouraging us to be strong and to persevere in prayer. She was so compassionate, even to "little people" like us. My sister, Ruthie, so touched by Mother Teresa's kindness and care, said: "No one showed more love than Mother Teresa."

Mother Teresa's thoughtfulness caught me off guard at times, because I was simply not expecting her to think of the little things she did, which were so meaningful to me: like writing individual letters to me and my sister, or autographing my piece of paper with "God bless you, M. Teresa," or giving me Miraculous Medals when she heard that my mother was suffering with cancer. It never even occurred to me that I could ask for these things. Hers was a *foreseeing* love. Her mercy and compassion were always ready to be expressed in some special way, without my even asking for them.

See! I will not forget you . . . I have carved you on the palm of My Hand . . . I have called you by your name . . . You are mine . . . You are precious to Me . . . I love you.

Isaiah

LDM

Mother House, Calcutta
9 December 1994

Dear Susan,

I received your letter and will surely add my prayers to yours and those of Ruthie that "what God has joined together, no man may put asunder", that is the marriage of Ruthie and Rob. I am so happy to hear that you are being a strong support to your sister in this difficult time. Be like Our Lady who stood near the Cross of Her suffering Son, all the while believing that the Resurrection would come. Jesus has promised to answer the persevering prayer of faith.

God bless you
Teresa mc

LDM

Mother House, Calcutta
9 December 1994

Dear Ruthie,

Your sister Susan wrote to me about the painful situation of your marriage with Rob. Please be assured of my prayers for you both. This is the time to love like Jesus, with the strength of Jesus. Jesus knew the pain of being rejected by those He loved best and had chosen. But it was for these very same people that Jesus shed His Precious Blood. Ask the Sacred Heart of Jesus to fill you with Jesus' own love for your husband -- so that forgiveness bring peace and faithfulness bring Rob back to you.

God bless you
Teresa mc

Letters written by Mother Teresa to my sister Ruthie and me.

Leaving Calcutta a Little Bit Brighter

*What you can do, maybe I can't do ... and what I can
do, maybe you can't do. But together we can do something beautiful for God.*
MOTHER TERESA

A delightful surprise for me in Calcutta was having the opportunity to do art work for Mother Teresa and the Poorest of the Poor.

It all started as a simple wish. As the summer months were ending
and it was almost time for me to return home to the United States, I felt
very strongly that I wanted to leave something joyful with the children
and the poor men and women I would be leaving behind. Soon I would
be taking away my "hands to serve and heart to love," and I felt a great
deal of sadness about this. In the evenings, I began to create a special
painting for each of the two shelters: a brightly colored painting of the
words "I love you" for the orphanage, and a drawing of two outstretched
hands with words of prayer "Shine through us" for the sick and dying.

I approached Mother Teresa at the Motherhouse one evening to
show these paintings to her. She gave me permission to hang them in
their respective homes. Then she surprised me by asking for a personal
favor. She asked me to do two more drawings for her personally, and
she told me exactly what she wanted. This was a real deepening of my
friendship with the person I had admired so much from afar. I worked
diligently on these drawings in the evenings in my room. With great
care, I drew a little child in the palm of God's Hand. The picture was
accompanied by some words from Scripture that Mother Teresa cherished, words God had spoken to each of us through the prophet Isaiah:
See! "I will not forget you.... I have carved you on the palm of my
hand (Is 49:15-16). I have called you by your name. You are mine. You
are precious to me. I love you" (Is 43:1,4).

Before I had this drawing permanently framed, I wanted to show
it to Mother Teresa to see if she wanted me to make any changes in it.

She took the drawing out of my hand, reached for my pencil, and
began to write on it. I was filled with a sudden sense of panic, for I
thought she was going to ruin my sketch! Then I came to my senses
and realized: this is *Mother Teresa*! She can do *anything* to this drawing,

even scribble on it, and it will become much more precious, just by having been touched by her! I watched her movements and I was deeply moved by what she added to my work. On each of the five fingers of God's Hand, she wrote the words that Jesus had spoken: "You did it to me" (Mt 25:40). These words had meant so much to me because they are at the heart of her work. This drawing suddenly became infinitely more meaningful and precious to me, and I simply could not part with it. It had been created by me and Mother Teresa *together*! (I even wrote both of our names on the bottom of it.) So, I stayed up very, very late that night and made an exact duplicate of this drawing for her to keep;

I even reproduced the words she had written on the fingers of God's Hand. I gave the duplicate to Mother Teresa and I brought the original drawing home with me to share with others. Mother Teresa would show this drawing to people and point to the little child in the palm of God's Hand and say: "See this little child? This child is YOU! This is how much God loves you, how tenderly He holds you and protects you...."

Mother Teresa was very happy with what she received, and I could not have been more pleased.

My drawing of the child in the palm of God's Hand, as requested by Mother Teresa.

The Old Testament words Mother Teresa asked me to write on my drawing were very dear to her heart. She spoke about this verse on various occasions, using it to explain how precious each one of us is to our heavenly Father: "We need prayer to understand God's love for us," she said. "You have to read that beautiful passage in Isaiah where

God speaks and says: 'I have called you by name. You are mine.... I will give up nations for you. You are precious to me' [Is 43:1,3]. We are precious to Him. That man dying in the street — precious to Him. That millionaire — precious to Him. That sinner — precious to Him. Because He loves us."[12]

Painting the Walls of the Orphanage

When I hung the "I love you" painting in the orphanage, I stood back to see how it looked. The sight of this fresh, new painting against the old, dilapidated walls was terribly unsatisfying to me, but it gave me an idea. I wondered if the Sisters would allow me to paint the walls of the orphanage. I asked if I could paint a big "Number Train" on the walls. Rather than rejecting my idea, Sister Olga responded: "Maybe you could paint the ABCs as well!"

First, the holes in the walls had to be plastered and the rough spots had to be sanded down. Then a brilliant blue border was painted all around the orphanage, halfway up to the ceiling. As soon as the blue border was painted all around the orphanage walls, I started outlining my "Number Train" with chalk and then painted 10 puffs of smoke, 9 bumble bees, 8 raindrops, 7 ants, 6 balloons, 5 balls being juggled,

Creating a memory: The painting of the "Number Train" at the Children's Home.

(and a purple cow!) — all the way to the caboose. On some days, I sat on my bench painting for up to eleven hours straight; the hours passed very quickly because I absolutely loved what I was doing and for whom I was doing it. It was so rewarding to see the exuberant reaction of the children as their home became brighter by the day. Both the children and the walls came to life! The little ones would come up to me as I was painting and they would pull at my sleeve and say "Auntie! Auntie!" and then they would count the ten puffs of smoke for me. One little boy came up to me and started showing me how he could make the sound and movements of a train.

The children would take visitors by the hand and lead them to the sections of the orphanage where they could show them the freshly painted murals. Seeing the joy and pride they felt about their "new" home served as my generous compensation.

The ABCs

My time was quickly running out, so I had to work from morning until evening on painting the ABCs in order to finish the project before leaving Calcutta. I could not bear to leave the orphanage with only half of a train or half of the alphabet! Even though the general rule is that all the volunteers must leave the Children's Home at lunch time when the children take their naps, I was allowed to stay and work because of these special circumstances. As I worked on the painting, I could look

"A" for apple, "B" for bear and balloons, "C" for child . . .

over my shoulder and see all the little ones in their cribs behind me. The most heartwarming part of all was when I heard one of the little children quietly singing "A, B, C, D...." I glanced back and watched a tiny girl in her crib pointing her finger at each of the letters as she was softly singing. I could see and hear for myself that this work would bring much color and song into their lives.

"Let the Children Come to Me"

I asked Mother Teresa if there was anything special she would like me to paint on the walls of the children's orphanage. Naturally, she wanted something a little more religious. We chose a Scripture passage from Luke, Chapter 18, which happens to be one of my personal favorites: "Jesus ... said: 'Let the children come to Me, and do not hinder them; for the kingdom of God belongs to such as these.' "

This was the original painting I did at Mother Teresa's request. Five years later, I returned to Calcutta and I saw that these paintings were still on the walls of the orphanage, but the original work had been touched up quite a bit over the years. These murals did not exhibit any artistic talent, but they made the children very happy!

Mother Teresa's Portrait

The sight of her, or even the thought of her, always gives me a great feeling of happiness.
MALCOLM MUGGERIDGE

Much to my delight, one painting project led to another. When Sister Luke heard that I was painting the walls of the Children's Home and making drawings for Mother Teresa, she wanted me to do a favor for her as well. She led me upstairs to the roof of the Home for the

Dying and showed me a large circular cement "block" on which a half-deleted portrait of Mother Teresa remained. Sister asked me to re-paint Mother Teresa's face with this simple prayer: "Be with Mother through life's journey" — a prayer for Mother's safety as she traveled throughout the world on her various missions.

Since this special project was undertaken up on the roof of the Home for the Dying, directly above the men's section, I could peer down through the windows at the men lying lifelessly in the rows of stretcher beds below. To the right of me, I could see all the domes of the Kali Temple. All around me were the unusual sounds and smells of the busy streets of Kalighat below. It was like being on a small mountaintop. I was in my own little world as I painted. As soon as I finished my painting for the day, however, I had to return to the hectic, chaotic world below.

Mother Teresa's Prayer
in the City Hall, Brisbane
15 October 1981

"Jesus living in my heart, I believe in your faithful love for me. I love you."

Left: I stood for hours at a time painting in the sweltering hot sun, praying. Whatever the outcome of this portrait of Mother Teresa, there was nothing like the real thing. *Right:* Sister Luke gave me a small prayer card (dated 1981) with a photograph of Mother on it; this is what I used to do the painting.

By the grace of God, I was able to finish every single art project that I had begun: the two original paintings, the Number Train, the ABC's, a picture on the orphanage wall for Mother Teresa, two special drawings for Mother Teresa, and the portrait on the roof of the Home for the Dying. I was grateful that I was able to accomplish all of these in just a couple of weeks.

Part III

❧

Mother Teresa's Spiritual Lessons

Chapter Four

The Secrets of Mother Teresa's Sanctity

$\mathscr{I}$ finally made it to the little, unnoticeable alleyway in which the entrance of the Motherhouse is located. Without exact directions, I would never have found it! Walking slowly down this narrow, muddy passageway, I noticed the faces and bodies of people at their gray doorsteps. Their worn, dirty appearances blended in with the walls of the buildings. On the right-hand side of this alley, I found a rust-colored door with a wooden cross on it. It was marked with the name "MOTHER TERESA, M.C." and the number "54A." I had found the Motherhouse!

My diary, June 1986: *The Motherhouse is the world headquarters for the Missionaries of Charity. It is where Mother Teresa lives in Calcutta. On my first day in Calcutta, I simply showed up at her doorstep. I was greeted at the door by a couple of young Sisters who escorted me to the stairs leading up to Mother Teresa's office area and the chapel. Every day at the Motherhouse I would pass by a sign with Mother Teresa's words: "Be kind. I prefer our Sisters to make mistakes through kindness rather than to work miracles through harshness and unkindness."*

Everything Starts with Prayer

My secret is quite simple. I pray.
MOTHER TERESA

When I first arrived in Calcutta, Mother Teresa was in the United States. Thus, my first weeks in India were without her. During that time, I settled into a very meaningful routine — attending Mass at the Motherhouse in the early morning, volunteering in the children's orphanage until noontime, serving in the Home for the Dying every afternoon until about 6 p.m., and then attending a Holy Hour of prayer in Mother Teresa's convent chapel every evening. At Mass, I even settled into a particular place where I knelt each morning, just inside the doors of the chapel, against the back wall facing the altar. I did not realize that my special place of prayer was right beside Mother Teresa's place until she returned from overseas and appeared one morning kneeling on the floor right beside me. What a happy surprise that was!

"For my house shall be called a house of prayer for all peoples" (Is 56:7). All people were welcome to join the Sisters in prayer and worship at the Motherhouse. The chapel was a simple and beautiful place. There were no pews, chairs, or cushions. Everything in Mother Teresa's life seemed to be stripped down to the bare essentials. Each day, dozens of volunteers and hundreds of Sisters would gather together in prayer. We would each remove our sandals and enter the chapel barefoot. This was the custom in Mother Teresa's chapel, for we were stepping onto holy ground, into God's presence. Sometimes while we were praying in this chapel at Mother Teresa's house, it seemed as if heaven was just upstairs from where we were, and there was nothing blocking the way

On the first level, there was a small, open courtyard. Here, the Sisters could be seen from the second-story balcony scrubbing their saris[13] in pails of sudsy water. Upstairs, on the second level, there was an open balcony overlooking this same courtyard. This is where the chapel is located. Our time of prayer in this chapel was one of the great highlights of my experience in Calcutta.

or keeping us from going up. We were free to go there spiritually, through prayer, with faith and love.

During the times of prayer in the chapel, we would sit and kneel on the open cement floor. The windows overlooking the streets below were always open, and this was both a blessing and a curse: it let in any breeze that there might be to relieve us in the stifling heat as we prayed; but the street noises were so loud that we often could not hear the priest as he celebrated Mass each morning. How I longed to be able to hear the beautiful readings from Scripture, but all I heard was the competing sounds of loud horns, screeching crows, human voices, and clanging trams.

Mother Teresa and her missionaries throughout the world begin every day with prayer and Holy Mass, because to see Christ "requires that you pray." She said: "In the Eucharist, I see Christ in the appearance of bread. In the slums, I see Christ in the distressing disguise of the poor.... That is why this work becomes possible." Without Christ, "I could do nothing."

As Mother Teresa would remind us, "Everything starts from prayer. Without asking God for love, we cannot possess love and still less are we able to give it to others." Our days began with prayer, ended with prayer, and were filled in between with prayer. Mother Teresa even used to encourage us to "pray the work," to contemplate God and the things of heaven even as we kept our hands busy here on earth.

Turning to God first was Mother Teresa's way of doing things. We all tried to follow her example. When we entered the Home for the Dying each day, for instance, we never touched a single person, we never helped a single person, until we first stopped and prayed together. We would ask God for all the strength, peace, kindness, understanding, love, and everything we needed to serve our brothers and sisters who were suffering and dying. Then we would go about our work.

Dearest Lord, the Great Healer, I kneel before You
since every good and perfect gift must come from You.
I pray, give skill to my hands, clear vision to my mind,
kindness and sympathy to my heart.

Give me singleness of purpose, strength to lift at least a part of
the burden of my suffering fellowmen,
and a true realization of the privilege that is mine.
Take from my heart all guile and worldliness
that with the simple faith of a child I may rely on You. Amen.

Holy Eucharist Was Mother Teresa's Daily Spiritual Nourishment

Jesus explained: "I am the bread of life.... If anyone eats this bread, he shall live forever."
JOHN 6:35, 51

Mother Teresa's whole life testified to her intense love and devotion to Christ and her deep faith in Him. She could not go a single day without the Presence of Jesus, without Holy Eucharist. Every day, she prayed: "Oh Jesus! Grant that You may be the object of our thoughts and affections, the subject of our conversations, the end of our actions, the model of our life, our support in death, and our reward eternally in Your heavenly kingdom."

"His love in action for us was the crucifixion. That's why we begin the day with Mass, with Holy Communion. That gives us the strength and the courage and the joy and the love to touch Him, to love Him, to serve Him. Without Him, we couldn't do it. With Him, we can do all things," Mother Teresa said.[14]

Mother Teresa always took Our Lord at His Word, and this explains her profound reverence and humility in receiving Holy Eucharist. Through the eyes of faith, she could always see that she was receiving the Sacred Body of Christ[15] during Holy Communion. On my very first day at Mass in the chapel at the Motherhouse, I experienced something that has had a lasting influence on my life and faith. When it came time for Communion, I noticed that the Sisters proceeded in single file and, as they approached the altar, one by one, they bowed, deeply and reverently. I had never seen this before and I wondered why they were doing this. It looked as if they were bowing before a king. As I pondered this, I suddenly realized that they were bowing because they *were* before a king! They were about to receive the King of kings! The humility, love, and reverence with which they each received the Body of Christ had a profound impact on me. Previous to this experience, as I would approach the altar during Holy Communion, I seemed to have different thoughts in my mind. But after witnessing Mother Teresa and her Sisters, I was filled with a deep and lasting awareness of the One I was about to receive in Holy Communion. I perhaps do not bow as obviously as these missionaries do, but in my heart, I bow. In my heart, I am aware of the most priceless gift I am about to receive. I realize that I am approaching the Savior of the world.

When Mother Teresa returned to Calcutta from the United States, she attended Mass every day with us. She would lead us in saying prayers and she would also help the priest to distribute Holy Eucharist. This was one of my favorite experiences in Calcutta — receiving the Body of Christ from the hands of a living saint.

On that first morning, as I approached the altar and realized that Mother Teresa was serving as the Eucharistic Minister at the head of my line, my heart started racing uncontrollably. As soon as I got back to my place and knelt on the floor after receiving Holy Eucharist, my gratitude came pouring out in a flood of tears. Not only had Mother Teresa's hand touched my lips, but as I knelt in prayer on the floor, I held the Son of God in my soul.

One of the most beautiful and moving things to witness was Mother Teresa in prayer — her intense love as she silently spoke with and listened to God. It seemed like a holy communion of hearts: her heart and the heart of God. One could see the radiance of her whole being. As one Sister said so beautifully: "When we see her praying, we feel like praying."[16]

Mother Teresa taught us that we must prepare our hearts for the sacred privilege of receiving Holy Eucharist, which is nothing less than a most intimate communion with God. Our hearts should not be filled with distractions and impurities as we approach the altar, but should instead be pure, simple, focused, filled with joy, and ready for this most blessed encounter. Sincere confession and prayerful self-examination are effective means of preparation. But Mother Teresa taught us that if we can see, as we approach the altar, that our hearts are not fully ready to receive Holy Eucharist, the supreme Love-Gift, then we should have recourse to Our Blessed Mother, Mary. Mother Teresa went so far as to say that we should ask the Mother of God for her heart! The heart of Mary was the most faithful, most pure, and most pleasing to God. Mother Teresa inspired me to just go ahead and ask her for her heart with the faith and loving confidence of a child. She taught me the following prayer:

Photo provided to author by Mother Teresa

Oh Mary, Mother of Jesus, give me your heart,
so beautiful, so pure, so immaculate,
so full of love and humility,
that I may be able to receive Jesus in the Bread of Life,
love Him as you love Him, and serve Him
in the distressing disguise
of the Poorest of the Poor. Amen.

Mother Teresa reminded me in a letter that, "We become full of grace each time we receive Jesus in Holy Communion.... Let us thank God for all His graces." Each of the Holy Sacraments is an encounter with God. Mother Teresa's chapel — where we adored and received the Most Blessed Sacrament of all — was like a holy mountain. It was a place of meeting with our almighty and ever-loving God. After being filled with His Real Presence, we could go back out onto the streets, knowing that God was with us at every step.

The Power of Turning to God

Look to him ... and be radiant.
PSALMS 34:6

We were able to keep our spirits up and keep loving and serving because we kept turning to God. "Our lives, to be fruitful, must be full of Christ," Mother Teresa said. "To be able to bring His peace, joy, and love, we must have it ourselves, for we cannot give what we have not got." This requires that we spend time with God, look at Him, open our hearts to Him, and empty our hearts of all that is not Him.

As we prayed in Mother Teresa's chapel, we always faced the tabernacle on the altar. The tabernacle is the special cabinet in church where the Most Blessed Sacrament, the sacred Body of Christ, is kept. It is for this reason that my father always taught us to bless ourselves whenever we passed a Catholic church. Our Sign of the Cross was a sign of acknowledgment and love as we passed by God's house. In her writings, Mother Teresa compared this sanctuary to our human hearts. She said: "A Christian is a tabernacle of the living God. He created me, He chose me, He came to dwell in me, because He wanted me. Now that you

Kneeling before the Blessed Sacrament was like kneeling before the window to heaven. We received countless graces during these times of prayer. I always felt imbued with peace when I left Mother Teresa's chapel. It is one of my favorite places on Earth. In the words of an old peasant to Saint John Vianney, "I just look at God and God looks at me."

know how much God is in love with you, it is but natural that you spend the rest of your life radiating that love."

Exactly as with Mass each morning, all were welcome to join the Missionaries of Charity at a Holy Hour of Adoration and silent prayer every evening. We would all kneel on the floor facing the simple altar in the candle-lighted chapel. We would pray the Rosary together, and then kneel in silence for the remainder of the time. The Most Blessed Sacrament was exposed within a gold monstrance for all to gaze upon and adore.[17]

Each Holy Hour was a time of peace, reflection, and thanksgiving. For those of us who were Catholic, this daily hour of adoration was a priceless opportunity we all treasured. It was one of the many highlights of each day. For those who were not Catholic, it was a tremendous source of peace, a time of spiritual and emotional renewal, a time of silent meditation. Mother Teresa and countless Sisters and visitors had prayed in that chapel for many years. So much prayer, love, and adoration have risen to heaven from that chapel that it has become a holy place where God is present.

"Love to pray," Mother Teresa said, "for prayer gives a clean heart. And a clean heart can see God." I always felt that the look on her face revealed that she was contemplating God and she was very sensitive to His presence within her heart. It was a look of deep peace, meditative moments, as though there was Someone on her mind.

One evening, during a beautiful time of deep prayer and reflection, my Grampa came to mind during the last few minutes of prayer. He had passed away three years earlier and yet I was struck with the clear and sud-

My Irish Grampa used to call me his Susie when I was a young girl. Even though he was already in heaven when I made my journey to India, I felt in my heart that he was somehow responsible for my meeting Mother Teresa. And the book contract for getting this story published "just happened" to be written on his birthday. He had a profound impact on my spirituality as I was growing up, and yet I never heard him say a single word about spiritual matters. He didn't need to.

den realization that he was very much responsible for this beautiful experience I was having in Calcutta. It is as if he had been praying for me and helping me, watching over "his girl." I realized that he was looking down on me lovingly, proudly, prayerfully, like a sparkling, glimmering strand of love from heaven to me. How I wanted God to bless my dear grandfather's soul and let him know that I loved him dearly. I could feel his presence, warmth, and love.

Mother Teresa wanted us to grow in our desire to pray. She encouraged us to feel the need for prayer and to take the trouble to pray every day. "Prayer enlarges the heart and makes it capable of containing God's gift of Himself," she said. "Ask and seek, and your heart will grow big enough to receive Him and keep Him as your own." She taught us that "the more you pray, the more you will love to pray; and the more you love to pray, the more you will pray."

We Need to Quiet Ourselves

Souls of prayer are souls of great silence.
MOTHER TERESA

"God speaks in the silence of our hearts, and we listen," Mother Teresa taught us. In order to hear him, we need to be still, we need silent prayer. Perhaps we could not find any outward silence in this city of clamor and chaos, but it was important for us to find an inward silence, a silence of the heart, in order to be renewed, recreated, and refreshed each day. Mother Teresa would remind us so beautifully and so humbly that her great "secret" to the awe-inspiring fruitfulness of her life was simply that she prayed.

Through prayer, Mother Teresa was filled with enough grace to touch the "untouchables" of society. "Prayer changes our hearts," Mother Teresa said. It makes us capable of doing things we never thought possible.

Mother Teresa's teachings on prayer were simple and practical, yet powerful and true. Her "secret" should not be a secret at all:

> The beginning of prayer is silence. . . . God speaking in the silence of the heart. And then we start talking to God from the fullness of the heart. And He listens.

The beginning of prayer is Scripture . . . we listen to God speaking. And then we begin to speak to Him again from the fullness of our hearts. And He listens. That is really prayer. Both sides listening and both sides speaking.[18]

To be able to pray we need a pure heart. With a pure heart we can see God. We need a pure heart to love Jesus and to live His life ... whatever He chooses for our life. It is not we who live; it is He who has to live in us. Allowing Him to live His life in us is prayer. And the more we allow Him, the more we grow in likeness of Christ.[19]

Prayer, to be fruitful, must come from the heart and must be able to touch the heart of God. See how Jesus taught His disciples to pray. Call God your Father, praise and glorify His name. Do His will, ask for daily bread, spiritual and temporal. Ask for forgiveness of your own sins and that we may forgive others — and also for the grace to be delivered from evil which is in us and around us.... Perfect prayer does not consist in many words, but in the fervor of the desire....[20]

The energy of God will be ours to do all things well. The unity of our thoughts with His thoughts, the unity of our prayers with His prayers, the unity of our actions with His actions, of our life with His life. All our words will be useless, unless they come from within — words which do not give the light of Christ increase the darkness.[21]

"God is the friend of silence," Mother said. "We need to find God, but we cannot find Him in noise, in excitement. See how nature, the trees, the flowers, the grass grow in deep silence. See how the stars, the moon and the sun move in silence. The more we receive in our silent prayer, the more we can give in our active life. Silence gives us a new way of looking at everything. We need this silence in order to touch souls. The important thing is not what we say but what God says to us and what He says through us." Mother Teresa could not emphasize enough that "there is no life of prayer without silence.[22]

Mother Teresa wrote to me and encouraged me: "Silence your heart and mind of all useless desires and distractions, so you may be able to listen to Him in the silence of your heart. You will then know for certain what He wants of you. I pray for you … and I hope you pray for me also." Mother advised me to empty my heart of what is useless because "even God Himself cannot fill what is already full" (August 6, 1990).

A month later, Mother Teresa again reminded me of the importance of quieting my heart and taking time to pray. She wrote: "I pray for you that you silence all other desires so you may listen to His voice in the silence of your heart. Make time for God in your daily life — to be still and know He is God. I am sure you love Him.…"

Mother Teresa taught us: "The more united we are to God, the greater will be our love and readiness to serve the poor wholeheartedly. Much depends on this unison of hearts. Today, more than ever, we need to pray for the light to perceive the word of God, for the love to accept the will of God, for the way to do the will of God."

"The more we receive in silent prayer, the more we can give in our active life," Mother said. We need to practice the silence of humility, the silence of the eyes, of the ears, of the tongue. "If we don't have that silence, then we don't know how to pray."

Some Prayers Mother Taught and Prayed

Mother Teresa wrote this inscription inside one of her little prayer books that she gave me:

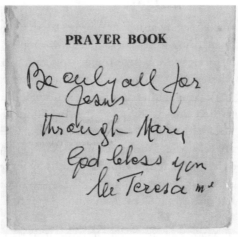

"Be only all for Jesus through Mary. God bless you. Mother Teresa, M.C."

lother Teresa prayed the following prayers every single day — and as a friend exclaimed to me: "If they were good enough for Mother Teresa, they're a hundred times better and more necessary for me!"[23]

Anima Christi

Soul of Christ, sanctify me.
Body of Christ, save me.
Blood of Christ, inebriate me.
Water from the side of Christ, wash me.
Passion of Christ, strengthen me.
O Good Jesus, hear me.
Within Thy Wounds, hide me.
Suffer me not to be separated from Thee.
From the malicious enemy, defend me.
At the hour of my death, call me, and bid me come unto Thee,
that with Thy saints I may praise Thee, forever and ever. Amen.

Mother encouraged me to "share the following prayer with my circle of friends and it would bring them peace and joy, too." She said: "We pray this prayer every day after Holy Communion, because it is very fitting for each one of us."

Prayer for Peace

Lord, make me a channel of Your peace, that where there is hatred, I may bring love; where there is wrong, I may bring the spirit of forgiveness; where there is discord, I may bring harmony; where there is error, I may bring truth; where there is doubt, I may bring faith; where there is despair, I may bring hope; where there are shadows, I may bring light; where there is sadness, I may bring joy. Lord, grant that I may seek rather to comfort than to be comforted; to understand than to be understood; to love than to be loved; for it is by forgetting self that one finds; it is by forgiving that one is forgiven; and it is by dying that one awakens to eternal life. Amen.

Every day at Mass, Mother Teresa led us in this prayer.

Prayer of Pope Paul

Make us worthy, Lord, to serve our fellow men throughout the world who live and die in poverty and hunger.

Give them through our hands this day their daily bread, and by our understanding love, give peace and joy.

Throughout each day, we did our best to bring these words to life. Mother Teresa believed so firmly in Christ's merciful *love* for each one of us — and she helped us to experience this love as well, by being a channel of it and by leading us to the Source. She taught us this simple aspiration: "Dear Jesus, in my heart, I believe in Your tender, faithful love for me. I love You."

Even Saints Need Prayers

I was amazed to hear Mother Teresa ask for *my* prayers. One might think that someone as holy as she does not need *our* prayers — rather, we need *her* prayers! But I have learned through this experience that even saints, and perhaps *especially* saints, need prayers. And she asked for them very often:

Let us pray for *each other* that in us and through us God may be glorified (Mother Teresa to me, January 9, 1988).

Be certain of my prayers for you and especially for the little children you care for (at the Maine Children's Cancer Program). Please pray for me. . . (Mother Teresa to me, June 1988).

Please pray much for Mother (Mother Teresa to me, October 8, 1990).

When I read the following words by Mother Teresa, they took me by surprise: "I don't think there is anyone else who needs God's help and grace more than I do. I feel so forsaken and confused at times! And I think that's exactly why God uses me: because I cannot claim any credit for what gets done. On the contrary, I need His help twenty-four hours a day. And if days were longer, I would need even more of it." These words give me great comfort, for even Mother Teresa of Calcutta sometimes felt forsaken and confused.[24] Somehow this gives me strength and courage in my own weakness and times of uncertainty. She taught us by her example to rely so much on faith — to trust in God Who helps us "twenty-four hours a day."

Living Our Faith — So That We Need No Words

Mother Teresa did not need to talk about her faith. We could *see* it. We just needed to look at her life and ways. She did not need to speak about love. She was living it. She "preached without preaching, not by words, but by her example ... by the evident fullness of the love her heart bore for Christ."[25] I have so much respect for those who do not need to use words to share their faith and witness to God's tender love and mercy. The example of Mother Teresa's life was more eloquent than any words that could be spoken. She was like the hands, heart, and voice of Jesus on earth.

Her unshakable faith was at the very heart of all her endeavors: In her own words, she practiced: "Faith in Christ Who has said: 'I was hungry, I was naked, I was sick, and I was homeless ... and you did

Mother taught us this simple aspiration: "Dear Jesus, in my heart, I believe in Your tender, faithful love for me. I love You." Mother speaking to my friend, Jane Clement.

that to Me' [Mt 25:42,43]. On these words of His all our work is based." Mother always took Christ at His Word; her work and her entire life were built on the solid rock of Divine Wisdom and Our Lord's promises.

Another prominent cornerstone of Mother Teresa's spirituality, which was a powerful, beautiful, and often untold part of her life, was her devotion to Mary, the Blessed Mother of God.

The Blessed Mother of God Was a "Cause of Joy" to Mother Teresa

One of Mother Teresa's great secrets of sanctity was her nearness to the Blessed Virgin Mary, whom she loved beyond telling. She called her, "The most beautiful of all women, the greatest, the humblest, the most pure, the most holy ... a model for all women." She is "the spotless mirror of God's love."

Mother Teresa's devotion to Mary was evident in so many ways. For example, the gift she most often gave wherever she went was a Miraculous Medal, with the image of Mary on it. She also handed out rosary beads (another great article of devotion to the Virgin Mary) to countless individuals. Even in the constitution of the Missionaries of Charity, inspired in large part by Mother Teresa herself, it states that their Society is "dedicated to the Immaculate Heart of Mary, Cause of our Joy and Queen of the World. We honor Her by praying the rosary with love and devotion and by radiating Her humility, kindness, and thoughtfulness towards others." The Blessed Virgin Mary played a prominent role in the spirituality of Mother Teresa. She was the perfect model of faith and love, whom Mother Teresa sought to imitate and taught others to imitate. Mother personally encouraged me to "Keep very close to Our Lady."

Mother Teresa loved how the Blessed Virgin Mary, with Jesus Christ in her womb, "went in haste" through the rugged hill country of Judea as soon as she found out that her cousin Elizabeth was expecting a child in her old age. Mary is the model of all Christians in this scene not only because she was practicing the most sublime virtue of charity, but also because she was bringing the very presence of Jesus with her, within her, to bring great joy and peace to the one whom she served. Mother Teresa loved how Our Lady always thought of the needs of others, like the young newlyweds at the wedding feast at Cana, where She told her Son that they had run out of wine. It was at her gentle prompting and because of her deep care for others that Our Lord performed His first public miracle. Mother Teresa sought to imitate all of Mary's beautiful virtues, her patient endurance, her eloquent silence, her humility, and her enduring love.

Pointing to Our Lady as a model for each one of us to follow, Mother Teresa said:

> Mary can teach us silence — how to keep all things in our hearts as she did, to pray in the silence of our hearts. Mary can teach us kindness.... Let us, like her, be aware of the needs of the poor, be they spiritual or material, and let us, like her, give generously of the love and grace we are granted. Mary will teach us humility — though full of grace, yet only the handmaid of the Lord, she stands as one of us at the foot of the Cross, a sinner needing redemption. Let us, like her, touch the dying, the poor, the lonely, and the unwanted according to the graces we have received and let us not be ashamed or slow to do the humble work.[26]

In a letter written to me just one day before my birthday in 1989, Mother Teresa said: "My gratitude is my fervent prayer for you that you may be humble like Mary so as to be holy like Jesus. Like Mary, let us be full of zeal to give Jesus to others. Like her, we too become full of grace each time we receive Jesus in Holy Communion."

One day in Calcutta I tried to give a bouquet of roses to Sister Priscilla to thank her for a special favor. She told me to give the whole bouquet to Mother Teresa, who was praying in the chapel at that moment. I went into the chapel and, bending down to her level, I offered my gift to Mother. She immediately pointed to a beautiful statue beside the altar and told me to present the whole bouquet to Our Lady! They were always thinking of others. Sister Priscilla was thinking of Mother Teresa, and Mother Teresa was unceasingly thinking of Our Blessed Mother. So, in the end, I presented my bouquet of roses to Our Lady by laying them at the foot of her beautiful statue ... and all three of us were delighted with this outcome.

In so many of Mother Teresa's letters to me, she gave testimony to her deep devotion to Mary. Her letters are filled with such a tender love for our heavenly Mother and unshakable confidence in her divine intercession. "Entrust yourself" to her, Mother Teresa said. "Cling" to her, "stay close" to her, "be like" her. "…always have a pure heart to see Jesus even in those who are not dying and do not seem to have any acute needs. May you always be a channel of His peace, His love, His truth, His mercy and His forgiveness. Keep very close to Our Lady, pray the Rosary every day, and allow her to lead you deeper into Jesus' Heart" (Mother Teresa's letter to me on Valentine's Day, 1989).

Mother Teresa often mentioned the Blessed Virgin Mary in her letters and words of advice:

> I am happy that you are well disposed and open to the will of God since that is of greatest importance in all we do. Cling to Mary and ask her to teach you how to love Jesus more and more since no one did the will of God as completely as she did. I will be praying for you, Susan, and asking Jesus to fill your heart with the joy of loving Him alone and then you can share that joy with all you meet beginning in your own family. Please pray much for Mother [Mother Teresa, in a letter to me, October 8, 1990].

> I ask Our Lady to give you her heart so beautiful, so pure, so loving, so humble, that you may be so empty of self like she was and love Him as she loved Him and serve Him as she did, keeping close to Him even at the foot of the Cross … [Mother Teresa to me, on January 6, 1990].

> Keep Mary very close to you, very close. Ask her again and again to be a Mother to you. I find this little prayer a great help, and when I need something … in advance I tell Our Lady: "Mary, Mother of Jesus, be a Mother to me now!" [*LOVE: A Fruit Always in Season*, p. 189].

> … I am praying for you, asking Mary, Our Lady of the Way, to give you the light to know God's will for you, for the courage to accept it, and for the love to do it, cost what it may!

Put your hand into the hand of Mary and ask her to help you
... [Mother Teresa to me, in February 1992].

... May Our Blessed Mother in her great love for you
help you grow in her likeness through humility of heart and
purity of life. She will see the needs of your heart too and will
tell you to do whatever He tells you. So continue to trust in
her love for you. Wait on God in prayer to discover His will
for you. Please be assured of my prayers for you ... [Mother
Teresa to me, December 30, 1992].

Let us ask Our Lady to make our hearts "meek and humble" as her Son's was. It is so very easy to be proud and harsh
and selfish — so easy; but we have been created for greater
things. How much we can learn from Our Lady! She was so
humble because she was all for God. She was full of grace.[27]

... Our Lady trusted God ... She said "yes" continually
with full trust and joy, trusting in Him without reserve.[28]

Pray especially to Our Blessed Mother Mary, placing all
your intentions into her hands. For she loves you as her Son.
She will guide you in all your relationships so that peace may fill
your life ... [Mother Teresa to me, December 1994].

... Ask her [Mary] to be a mother to you ... [Mother
Teresa to me, August 6, 1996].

... Let us entrust [our loved ones] to Our Lady's care. She
will obtain for them the graces they need. She is our Mother
indeed ... [Mother Teresa to me, August 8, 1997].

As Mother Teresa's life reveals beautifully, true devotion to Mary
"is a secure means of going to Jesus Christ, because it is very character-
istic of Our Blessed Lady to conduct us surely to Jesus" (Saint Louis de
Montfort). Our Lady never keeps souls just to herself. Her mission,
from the very beginning, has always been to bring Jesus to the world
and to bring the world to Jesus, our salvation.

In a letter to her co-workers, Mother told us to "keep close to
Mary, the Mother of Jesus and our Mother. She will guide and protect
you and keep you only all for Jesus. Let nothing and nobody ever sep-
arate you from the love of Jesus and Mary — it was at her pleading that

This photograph always makes me laugh. It looks as though I took a picture of myself and *taped* it onto a photograph of Calcutta! I do not appear to fit in.

I and several other volunteers are surrounded by dozens of little children in Mother Teresa's orphanage in Calcutta. The children were hungry to be loved, hungry to belong to someone. We did our best to feed them — with all our hearts!

Missionaries of Charity holding some of the little children in the courtyard at the orphanage on a beautifully sunny day in Calcutta.

In the summer of 1986, I painted several murals on the walls in the Children's Home in Calcutta. *Top:* My first mural in the Children's Home was a "Number Train," which actually wrapped around two walls. The children were delighted with the bright images, and I was delighted by their joy. *Right:* These are the ABCs I painted on one wall in the room where the children slept.

My simple painting of Jesus and His words, "Let the children come to Me," on a wall in Mother Teresa's orphanage in Calcutta.

In almost all of the photographs from Calcutta, I was smiling. Not in this one. It's one thing to mess up a painting of the ABCs; it is quite another thing to mess up a painting of Mother Teresa's face! I was incredibly nervous about this assignment, but I could not have been more grateful for it.

A delightful surprise for me in Calcutta was the opportunity to do artwork for Mother Teresa. After I showed Mother two pictures I had painted for the Children's Home and for the Home for the Dying, she asked me to do two more drawings for her, personally. Through the years I did other drawings for Mother, including these two.

Top Right: The drawing of the Blessed Virgin Mary with the outline of Albania in the background and the city of Tirana centered at the Blessed Mother's heart commemorates Mother Teresa's return from her first mission to her native Albania.

Bottom Right: The drawing I made for Mother Teresa of Our Blessed Mother Mary with the Divine Child Jesus within her heart. Just weeks before she died, Mother Teresa wrote me: "I am glad to let you know that I did receive your picture … it is still hanging on my wall…."

"From Mary's Virginal Blood & Heart, the Supreme Love-gift: Jesus-the-Eucharist"

At the end of my summer in Calcutta, I gave Mother Teresa the two drawings she had asked me to make for her — a little child resting in the palm of God's Hand with the words of the prophet Isaiah: "See, I will not forget you!" and the drawing of two outstretched hands with the prayer to Jesus: "Shine through us."

See! I will not forget you...
I have carved you
on the palm of My hand
I have called you
by your name.
You are mine.
You are precious to Me
I love you.

~ Isaiah ~

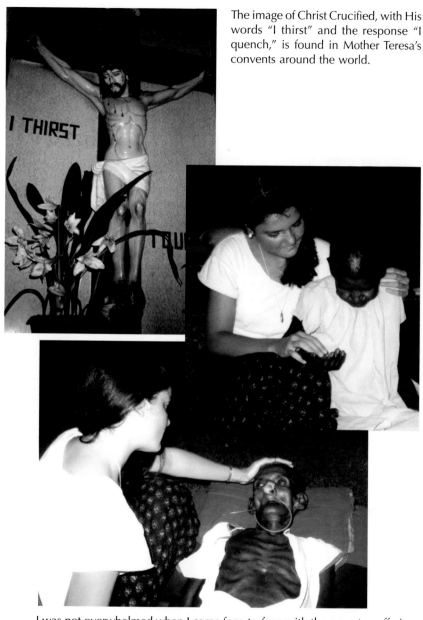

The image of Christ Crucified, with His words "I thirst" and the response "I quench," is found in Mother Teresa's convents around the world.

I was not overwhelmed when I came face-to-face with the poverty, suffering, disease, and death I found in Calcutta. I was expecting these things. But I was brought to tears by the incredible beauty I found amidst the ugliness of this city, the joy amidst the terrible suffering, the peace amidst the noise and confusion, and the life amidst the constant death. In this "hell on earth," I really experienced heaven.

THE GREATEST AIM
OF HUMAN LIFE
IS TO DIE
IN PEACE
WITH GOD

– MOTHER

Just six months prior to Mother Teresa's going home to God, a new Superior General was elected to lead the Missionaries of Charity. "Now I am happy," Mother said as she introduced her Indian-born successor to the world on March 14, 1997. Mother Teresa asked for everyone's support of Sister Nirmala, saying: "Pray so she can continue God's work."

Photo by Paul Amberg

Photo by Paul Amberg

Always a smile. No matter where in the world I have encountered Mother Teresa's Missionaries of Charity — whether in Calcutta, Rome, Paris, or New York City — they always have that distinguishing spirit of joy! This is amazing when one considers the austerity of their lives. In this photo, I'm speaking with Sister Nirmala, at her convent in Rome, October 1997.

Three Missionaries of Charity standing at the entrance of the Motherhouse in Calcutta. I have such a deep admiration for the way that the Missionaries of Charity live their lives and give their lives. They are sent all over the world, to the very poorest areas, to do God's work of love with great joy, humility, and grace. These Sisters *never* go back to comfortable homes or easy lives. Their sacrifices are lifelong, radical, and complete. What they give to Jesus is nothing less than everything.

The words on this page were the *very first words* I ever read by Mother Teresa. The simplicity, beauty, and truth in them were very appealing to me, and I found great inspiration in reading her words time and time again. I carried this page with me to Calcutta, and during one of my visits alone with Mother Teresa I pulled the folded, well-worn page from my pocket and showed it to her. She took it from me and said, "Oh, how colorful!" She then pulled out a pen and autographed it: "God bless you. M. Teresa, M.C." Instantly, this piece of paper became an even greater treasure to me. When I got home from Calcutta, I had it framed so that I could cherish it forever. Original illustration by Ted Lewin, used with his gracious permission.

A group of volunteers from Ireland, France, Australia, and America with Mother Teresa in the courtyard at the Motherhouse in Calcutta. Malcolm Muggeridge said: "Even if I were never to see Mother Teresa again, the memory of her would stay with me forever." I know exactly what he meant.

Mother Teresa introduced me to the Little Flower, and as a result, I came to translate some of Saint Thérèse's work from French into English. I was also blessed to meet Pope John Paul II and to present him with one of the books I helped translate.

Mother Teresa and Pope John Paul II shared their last earthly visit together in Rome in May 1997, and she was in Rome when she wrote to me on May 17. When I see this photograph of Mother Teresa holding hands with our Holy Father, I delight in believing that my written outpouring of gratitude was actually *with* her at that time!

"The meaning of our lives is to do all we can for the glory of God and the good of all people," Mother Teresa taught us. Mother holding hands with Pope John Paul II.

This picture of Mother Teresa and Pope John Paul II was hanging inside the Home for the Dying during the summer of my first visit in 1986.

Mother Teresa never liked being in front of a camera. She "offered up" to God the sacrifice of having her picture taken and asked that a soul would be saved for each photograph taken. If her wishes were honored, then countless souls have been saved by photographs of Mother Teresa alone! "I have said that if I don't go to heaven for anything else I will be going to heaven for all the publicity because it has purified me and sacrificed me and made me really ready to go to heaven," she said. She turned ordinary things of everyday life — like having her picture taken — into a prayer for the good of others. In this picture, Mother makes her way through a crowd of 5,000 after a special Mass at Our Lady, Help of Christians Church in Newton, Massachusetts, on June 15, 1995.

I never really understood the power, beauty, and deep meaning of the Holy Rosary until I learned to say it in Calcutta. We meditated on it every evening in the chapel with the Sisters, and often with Mother Teresa herself. The Sisters prayed the Holy Rosary everywhere they went, whether they were riding in the back of the ambulance through the streets of Calcutta or walking the streets of the South Bronx to visit shut-ins. For centuries, the Holy Rosary has been a powerful source of strength, sanctification, peace, and divine intervention for God's saints. "Pray the Rosary every day," Mother told me. I will carry with me always the memory of her gentle hands, as they are pictured here, with her rosary beads.

Mother Teresa welcomed anyone with "hands to serve and a heart to love" to join her in ministering to the Poorest of the Poor. Her life, which was inseparable from her faith, was founded on the words of Jesus: "For I was hungry and you gave me food, I was thirsty and you gave me drink, I was a stranger and you welcomed me, I was naked and you clothed me, I was sick and you visited me, I was in prison and you came to me…. Truly, I say to you, as you did it to the least of these my brethren, you did it to me" (Mt 25:35-36, 40).

the Society (the Missionaries of Charity) was born — let it be again at her pleading that the Society gives saints to Mother Church."

The Holy Rosary Is a Powerful Instrument of Grace

I never really understood the power, beauty, and deep meaning of the Holy Rosary until I learned to say it in Calcutta. We meditated on it every evening with the missionaries and often with Mother Teresa herself in the chapel. For Mother Teresa and many of the saints, the Rosary has been a powerful source of strength, sanctification, peace, and divine intervention.

Following Mother's example, the Sisters prayed the Holy Rosary everywhere they went — whether they were riding in the back of the ambulance through the streets of Calcutta, or walking the streets of the South Bronx to visit shut-ins. The Sisters even measured distance by the number of decades in the Rosary. Mother Teresa's missionaries' whole lives seem to revolve around Holy Eucharist and the Holy Rosary — around Our Lord Jesus and His Mother, Mary.

Mother Teresa taught us this prayer to Our Blessed Mother, which she had said every day (I have slightly adapted it):

"Immaculate Heart of Mary, Cause of our joy, pray for us, bless us, keep us in your most pure heart. Help us to do all the good we can so that we may please Jesus, through you, with you, and in you."

Chapter Five

❧

We Should Put Joy Into Everything We Do

JOY Is Half the Gift We Bring

Joy is strength. Joy is prayer. Joy is love.
MOTHER TERESA

I had thought a great deal about depression before going to Calcutta. It was a very important matter to consider. Not only would I be living in an overcrowded, desperately poor, struggling city, but I would be working every day in the Home for the Dying. I realized that it was very possible to become totally downcast by what I was about to encounter, but I knew that if I let myself fall into despair because of all the suffering and chaos, I would not be helping matters. I could not lift anyone else's spirits if my own were down. The last thing any poor, dying person needed was a depressed volunteer, wallowing in misery. So, I made a conscious decision not to allow myself to become depressed. I decided to concentrate on one human being at a time and to do all that I could for each one. Mother Teresa had taught me through her writings that joy is half the gift we bring. She believed that "we give *most* when we give with joy." She said: "We want to make [those who are suffering] feel that they are loved. If we went to them with a sad face, we would only make them much more depressed."[29] Wishing to bring as much joy, comfort, and peace as possible, I simply resolved to remain positive and happy.

In the event that my spirits did start to become weighed down while I was in India, I had a secret plan in my heart. As I walked the streets of Calcutta, I decided that I would sing some of my favorite songs. I would sing melodies that always filled my heart with joy: "Alleluia, Alleluia!"

and "Immaculate Mary." As it turned out, I did end up singing these songs, not because I needed them to lift my spirits, but rather because my spirits were so high that I wanted to sing to God!

During one of my visits alone with Mother Teresa, I sat down beside her on a little wooden bench outside her office. I had with me a folded piece of paper with a drawing of Mother Teresa and her beautiful words on JOY. My mother had sent it to me at college. Since these words had meant so much to me, I had carried them with me all the way to India. I unfolded the paper and showed it to Mother. She took it from my hand, and responded: "Oh! How colorful!" (In real life, her cheeks are not quite as rosy as they are in the painting!) Then she pulled out a pen and autographed it: "God bless you. M. Teresa, M.C." Instantly, this piece of paper became an even greater treasure to me. When I got home from Calcutta, rather than just taping it to the wall as I had done before, I had it framed so that I could cherish it forever. (Please see illustration in color section.)

"Do what you do with a happy heart," Mother Teresa would say. "Whenever you meet Jesus, smile at Him." In the background of the photograph is Howrah Bridge, which connects the two massive twin cities of Calcutta and Howrah. Deep in the slums of Howrah is one of Mother Teresa's orphanages.

We Experienced the Joy of Loving and Serving

The only ones among you who will be really happy are those who have sought and found how to serve.
ALBERT SCHWEITZER

The people around me in Calcutta were quite happy, and that helped to make mine a very positive experience. Prayer also filled our hearts with contentment. Mother Teresa used to say "joy is prayer," and we were praying throughout each day, even as we were serving the poor. Because of this, we were close to God throughout the entire summer. We carried Him in our hearts, and touched Him in the aching bodies of the destitute and dying. When God is with us, we have everything. This is what best explains our sense of happiness and deep fulfillment. We were letting God fill our hearts completely.

The work we did each day in the Home for the Dying and in the Children's Home made us content, too. In the words of Our Lord Jesus, "It is more blessed to give than to receive."[30] We experienced great fulfillment in trying to serve and give our best. It was clear that God cannot be outdone in generosity; we gave a little and received a lot.

"Joy comes to those who in a sense forget themselves and become totally aware of the other," Mother Teresa said. Through immersing ourselves completely in one person at a time in Calcutta — in the Home for the Dying particularly — we knew well the joy of sharing, the joy of giving a gift of self, the joy of total aware-

Photo by Michael Alexander, CNS

Joy was a big part of my experience in Calcutta, and it was especially apparent when Mother Teresa was around. She had a very playful nature; she never lost this beautiful quality, this youthfulness. She would talk to us, teach us, bless us, and make us laugh.

ness and love. This added much depth and duration to the joy that we experienced in Calcutta. "Keep the joy of loving God always in your heart, and share this joy with all you meet — and so become an instrument of peace," Mother taught the rich and poor alike.

The prayerful awareness of God's presence, the beautiful work we shared, and the people with whom I served were Calcutta's redeeming factors in my eyes. If it were not for the positive and uplifting human interactions and the intense spiritual aspect of this experience, I wonder if I would have found such peace and a real inner sense of contentment in this city that I refer to as hell on earth. I would have been calling Calcutta anything but beautiful.

It is amazing how love — even the love of one person like Mother Teresa — can transform a place like hell on earth into a place like heaven. Love makes such a difference. It seems that each one of us creates either heaven or hell on earth for those around us, by what we say and do, by what is in our hearts. We have the power to bring division and pain, or to bring peace and joy.

> My diary, June 22: *The men and the children squat in the gutter to wash themselves in the muddy water. They brush their teeth with sticks, old brushes, or simply their fingers. They lather up, and rinse off. They crouch down at the side of the road with elbows resting on their knees and arms dangling out in front of them. Some people are cooking breakfast, eating on the sidewalks, drinking hot tea — even in this heat. I, too, drink hot tea because I am told that since it is boiled, this water is no longer contaminated. The air is filled with thick smoke and strong fumes; I often find it difficult to breathe. I see, smell, hear, and feel so much: the drudgery, the rank odors, the incessant honking of horns, ringing of bells, chattering of voices; the heat and sweat, the greasy smoky air, the stares.*
>
> *Yet amidst it all, amidst all of the terribly unpleasant stimuli in these surroundings, I have sensed also the rich beauty underlying the ugliness and I have felt such contentment. It is the work. It is the human capacity for joy. It is the human element, the steady contact and the love. It is the Sisters, the other volunteers, the dying patients, and the orphaned children who reveal their untiring love of life. Their love of God and love of one another inspire me. Their joy sustains me.*

Men washing themselves in the gutters along a street in Calcutta.

I thought that I would be the one trying to rekindle the inner light of the destitute and abandoned people of Calcutta, of those I encountered in the "Black Hole," and share with them my own joy and love of life — as if they had none of that joy and love of their own. As it turned out, we lighted up one another's lives.

One afternoon in the Home for the Dying, I held a dying young man for hours. Later, as I stood outside the shelter, I felt a sense of fulfillment unlike any I had ever experienced before. If God had called me home to heaven, then and there, I could have accepted it peacefully, even joyfully and thankfully. I would not have put up a fight, because my heart was overflowing, my soul was so entirely satisfied. I could not have asked for more. I felt that I was experiencing a whole lifetime of fulfillment in those moments. I had been filled with total contentment, total peace, total life.

Joy Should Be the Compass that Leads Us

When Mother Teresa was trying to make the important decision about whether or not to enter the religious life, she asked a priest how she could know if this was, in fact, God's will or if it was simply her own will. His response to her has permanently impressed itself in my heart. The priest told Mother Teresa that *joy* should be the compass with which we make our life's decisions. If the thought of doing something brings us great joy and a deep sense of peace, then that is what God is calling us to do. If, on the other hand, the thought of doing something brings us anxiety and sadness or fills our souls with fear and hesitation, then most likely that is not what God is calling us to do. As Saint Paul wrote, the fruit of God's Holy Spirit is "joy, peace, patience, kindness, goodness, faithfulness, gentleness, self-control" (Gal 5:22-26). These are the "signs" that we should be following in life. They illuminate our paths. When we travel along well-illumined paths, we are free to run! If we are traveling along the wrong way, along a path darkened by hesitations, fears, and worries, then we are most likely not following God's will and we will be more likely to stumble and fall. We proceed with great slowness, and we do not have the confidence to run because we are unsure about whether we are even heading in the right direction. Since we live by the Spirit "…let us also walk by the Spirit" (Gal 5:25). This has been a great lesson in my life. It has helped to guide my steps, even through some very precarious situations. There have been times when I was being asked to take a giant leap of faith (into marriage, and into the religious life) and to make radical and permanently life-changing decisions. Since I could not make these decisions with great peace and happiness in my heart (I could only make them with anxiety), I decided not to take the plunge. This lesson has had a great impact on the course of my life, and I will treasure it always. I have learned that we should follow our peace. Follow our joy. Follow our hearts. For this is to follow our God. In addition to being guided by joy and peace, it is good to remember, most of all, to let love guide your life (Col 3:14). Love is perhaps the best compass of all, for "God is love."

It seemed clear that I was following my compass of love and joy as I continued this special journey.

Part IV

❧

Reflections on
Mother Teresa's Teachings

Chapter Six

God Is Disguised as the Poor, the Orphan, the Dying

*H*e "had no form or comeliness that we should look at him, and no beauty that we should desire him. He was despised and rejected by men; a man of sorrows, and acquainted with grief; and as one from whom men hide their faces he was despised, and we esteemed him not" (Is 53:2-3). This was prophetically written in Scripture about Jesus Christ, Who identified Himself so closely with the poor and outcast of society. Mother Teresa taught us to look at every dying derelict as Jesus Christ, the Son of God, Who Himself was "a man of sorrows, and acquainted with grief ... one from whom men hide their faces..." (Is 53:3). Jesus makes it easy for us to love Him. He identifies Himself

with the poor, the hungry, the little one, the least among us. He says that what we do unto these homeless, naked, hungry, outcast and little ones of the world, we do unto Him. The Son of God Himself said: "Truly, I say to you, as you did it to one of the least of these my brethren, you did it to me" (Mt 25:40).

When we give a glass of water to someone who is thirsty, when we receive a little child in His name, when we do anything with love for the least of humanity, we are loving God in the most beautiful and direct way. He makes it so easy for us to put our love for Him into living action. This is the whole foundation of Mother Teresa's life and work among the Poorest of the Poor. She said: "God is love. He loves you and me. If we love others as He loves us, it becomes evident that Christ is in the poor and lonely. The certainty of this reality is boundless for me."

Looking Beyond Appearances

I had so much respect for the way that Mother Teresa could look past the distressing outward appearances of people who were suffering and see human beings in need of love and understanding. There were people on the streets of Calcutta who were covered with open sores and wounds, infested with maggots, emaciated, filthy, and foul-smelling. Most of the passersby would not even *look* at them or go near them because it was so unpleasant to see their bodies like that. Most people would walk far around the bodies of the poor lying on the pavement, suffering. Even if some people looked at them, most would not go near them and certainly would not *touch* them.

Mother Teresa was not like most people. Not only did she look at those unfortunate beings, she approached them, touched them, and lifted them up out of the gutter. She cradled them in her arms and brought them to a place where they could be cared for; she bathed them, cleaned the maggots out of their open sores, fed them, gave them clean, dry garments to wear, gave them a bed to die in, and gave them love. She gave her whole heart, nothing less. She "loved until it hurt." To Mother Teresa, these were not *animals* suffering in the gutter. These were men, women, and little children. These were fellow *human beings*, created in the image and likeness of God, "created to love and to be loved." Each one was worthy of human dignity.

The most frightful human misery I saw in Calcutta was that of a woman with a gaping hole in the side of her face. When we fed her, the food would fall out of the hole in her face. I could see her cheekbone and her teeth through this hole. It was utterly disturbing and night-marish. There was also a woman in the Home for the Dying whose face had been burned completely. I was repulsed because her skin looked all melted. It took me three days before I could speak to her and look at her directly. I simply could not handle it at first. I had to be patient with myself as I learned to look at Jesus in "His most distressing disguise of the poor." I cannot imagine the emotional and physical pain that each of these women endured. And yet they were so resigned to what they had to bear. It seemed heroic to me.

The horrifying external appearances of the sick and destitute did not bother Mother Teresa. She looked into people's hearts. It seemed that she could see into souls. Mother Teresa had a tremendous ability to see Jesus in those who were suffering. She was able to do this because she was looking through the eyes of faith and the eyes of love.

I set out for India with the hope that I could somehow see past the upsetting appearances of Calcutta's poorest. I remember how I longed to be able to love as Mother Teresa loved. I also wished that I could watch Mother Teresa as she was shining her love on others, so that I could try to learn from her example and absorb all that I could. My greatest fear was that I might withdraw from the sick, dying, and poor people whom I had been embracing from afar. I worried that I would be repulsed by the actual sight of them. I thought that I might only see the frightening skeletal remains of human beings rather than the human beings themselves.

On my very first day in the Home for the Dying, I knew how I wanted to react to the sights I saw. This was my chance to put my wishes into action. I began to change the diaper-like cloths, clean up the messes, and distribute clean, dry smocks for the patients to wear; and, in time, I discovered other ways to serve and to lighten a little bit of their suffering. It was only in reaching out that I realized that I could begin to love as I dreamed of loving. One of the most powerful ways that Mother Teresa assisted me in loving the poor without paralyzing fear was by teaching me that in serving the poor, we were directly serving God. She often reminded us of Jesus' own words that *whatsoever we do to the least of humanity*, we do unto Jesus Himself. That made a tremendous difference. That explained why we were not afraid, but eager to serve in the Home for the Dying.

So many of the patients had conducted their lives on the sidewalk, scrounging for their food like animals. They had been unnoticed, uncared for, and unloved by all who walked past their bodies on the ground. In the Home for the Dying, the patients seemed truly amazed that someone was actually looking at them, taking time for them, caring for them in spite of their appearance. It was as if they had never experienced this before. I found the men to be so appreciative and deeply touched by having someone sitting by their bedside holding their hand. One of these men in particular looked up at me as I was caring for him, with so much feeling and emotion in his eyes. There was so much depth to his soul and to his suffering. So much depth to his gratitude. He seemed the most like Jesus to me. It was like Christ looking up at me and saying with his eyes: "You really understand who it is that you are touching." I was profoundly moved by this experience of touching this "untouchable" of society.

I loved the quiet, humble hearts of the poor. In their gentleness and humility, it was easy to recognize Jesus, Who was meek and humble of heart, and that was a very moving realization.

Staying Sensitive to the Poor

Although my volunteer work was primarily in the children's orphanage and in the shelter for dying destitutes, I tried not to lose sight of the needy people on the streets. I found that it was actually possible, with steady and intense exposure, to become desensitized to the suffering on the streets, because it was everywhere and so overwhelming. I needed to make a steady and conscious effort to remain sensitive to the human misery that I encountered outside the shelters. I bought bunches of bananas to share with the beggars I met. This practice compelled me to notice the unnoticed, and it kept me from becoming blind to what I saw every day. When I did not have any bananas left, I would try to at least acknowledge that the beggars were there. I would look at them, nod to them, smile at them, and reach out to touch them. It was less difficult to notice the poor and to make even the smallest gesture, than to turn my back on their suffering or struggle to avoid it.

And when I saw the struggles of the poor on the streets, I was inspired by the beautiful examples they set for me. For instance, as I was standing in front of a little cola shop drinking a fizzy "Thums Up" soda one afternoon when a beggar carrying her naked child approached me quietly, gesturing to me by putting her hand to her mouth. I reached into my pocket and handed her some rupees, which, I sensed, were like a jackpot to this desperate woman. She thanked me profusely. It was terribly hot and dry that day, and thinking that she might like to finish my soda and quench what must have been a torturous thirst, I handed her the bottle of cool "Thums Up." I stood in amazement as I watched her give every drop of it to her child and not one sip to herself. It reminded me of all the beautiful tales told by Mother Teresa about the real love and selfless giving that she constantly witnessed in the poor. This simple scene made me cry.

Sometimes I found people lying face down on the street and I would reach down and touch them and ask if they were all right. "Sometimes we meet Jesus rejected and covered in filth in the gutter. Sometimes we find Jesus stuffed into a drain, or moaning with pain from sores or rotting with gangrene, or even screaming from the agony of a broken back," Mother Teresa said. "The most distressing disguise calls for even more love from us" (*Saints Are Now*).

The Greatness of the Poor

We call them poor, but they are rich in love!
MOTHER TERESA

"The poor people are great people. They can teach us so many beautiful things," Mother Teresa said. "Maybe they have nothing to eat, maybe they have no home in which to live, but they are great people."

The poor give us a way of salvation because they give us a way of loving God. For this reason, Mother Teresa called them our "hope," our "love," and a gift to us. They provide us with a beautiful opportunity to put our love into living action. "The poor are God's gift," Mother said. "They are our love.... By their courage they truly represent the hope of the world. They have taught us a different way of loving God by making us do our utmost to help them." Mother Teresa felt that if people were convinced that the person lying in the dirt was truly their brother or sister, they would do something for that person. "People don't know what compassion is," she said. "They don't know people. If they understood, they would immediately realize the greatness of the people lying in the street and would simply love them. And the love would surely lead them to place themselves at their service."

Dearest Lord,
sow in me the spirit of this man —
that gentleness, that childlike innocence,
that quiet endurance, that profound humility,
that love.
"I offer You my heart.
Make it meek and humble, like Yours."

"We must acknowledge the dignity of the poor, respect them, esteem them, love them, serve them…. We owe a debt of gratitude to the poor…. They teach us by their faith, their resignation, their patience in suffering. They allow us to help them. And in doing so, we are serving Jesus." Mother Teresa, like no one else, instilled within our hearts a powerful awareness of what a *privilege* it is to serve the Poorest of the Poor.

Mother Teresa also reminded us that "the poor are human beings with feelings just like us." People should not look down on them. We are all children of God, worthy of love and human dignity.

"To serve the poor we must love them," Mother Teresa wrote. "In order to love the poor, we must first *know* them. And to know them means to know God. Then we must live with the poor; and to live with them means to live with God. Lastly, we must give our hearts in order to love them, and our hands to serve them, and this means to love God and serve Him."[31]

Photo by Paul Hulewicz

"Only in heaven will we see how much we owe to the poor for helping us to love God better because of them." Mother Teresa

Even though the conditions were so desperate, and most likely *because* they were so desperate, this is where Mother Teresa wanted to live, with the Poorest of the Poor:

> Oh God, through free choice and through Your love, I want to stay here and do Your will. No, I cannot go back. My community are the poor. Their security is mine. Their health is my health. My home is the home of the poor: not just of the poor, but of those who are Poorest of the Poor. Of those to whom one tries not to get too close for fear of catching something, for fear of the dirt, or because they are covered in germs and disease. Of those that do not go to pray because they can't leave their houses naked. Of those that no longer eat because they haven't the strength. Of those that fall in the streets, knowing that they are going to die, while the living walk by their sides ignoring them. Of those who no longer cry, because they have no tears left. Of the untouchables.[32]

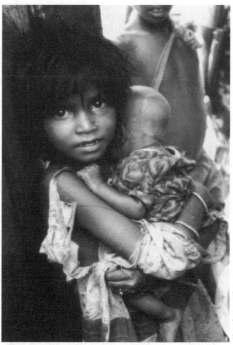

Even as we prayed in the chapel at the Motherhouse with all of the Sisters each day, morning and night, the loud clamor of the life of the poor on the streets below could be heard through the open chapel windows, reminding all of us why we were there and why we exist. It was very meaningful that, even as we were in prayer, the poor were close in mind and heart, and in every way.

"Today those who ignore or reject the poor, ignore or reject Christ. The poor do us the honor of allowing us to serve them." Mother Teresa

Mother Teresa knew that greatness comes from within. That is why she held her beloved poor of Calcutta in such great esteem. Her namesake, Saint Thérèse of Lisieux, knew this as well, as she wrote in her autobiography: "I understood true greatness is to be found in the soul, not in a name.... It is in heaven, then, that we shall know our titles of nobility. Then shall every man have praise from God and the one who on earth wanted to be the poorest, the most forgotten out of love of Jesus, will be the first, the noblest, and the richest!"

Mother Teresa had often told the story about a man whom the Sisters picked up from the drain, half eaten with worms, whom the Sisters brought to the Home for the Dying. Mother explained how this man was not bitter, but happy and grateful, knowing that he was going to die at least with someone loving him. Mother Teresa said: "And it was so wonderful to see the greatness of that man who could speak like that, who could die like that without blaming anybody, without cursing anybody, without comparing anything. Like an angel — this is the greatness of our people."

I found myself praying, as I sat at a patient's bedside, feeding him: "God, give me the heart of the poor. Give me this humility, give me this goodness, this gentleness, meekness, purity, and holiness. Give me this spirit of simplicity and total surrender. Give me this complete trust in You."

Every once in a while, as I stared into the eyes of one of the men who was closest to death, I could almost believe that I was looking into the eyes of Christ Himself, and that I was touching His broken, bruised, suffering body. It was such a privilege to be there.

"Every work of love brings a person face to face with God," Mother Teresa said.

Not only was my heart drawn to the silent ones, but I loved to serve them in silence. I would look into a dying man's eyes and he would look into mine, and we would say so much to each other *without any words*. Their eyes said so much to my heart. There was a deep communion, much deeper than with those who did much speaking.

Mother Teresa spoke of a dying man who said to one of the Sisters: "I am going home to God." Mother continued: "He did not say anything about his difficulties, only, 'I am going home to God.' Then he closed his eyes and went home. Just as simple and beautiful as that. He went home to Jesus. He went home to see the face of God. His heart was so pure and so beautiful. We don't realize the greatness of the poor and how much they give us. It is a wonder."[33]

Serving the Dying Is a Privilege

Scripture tells us: "...for the LORD sees not as man sees; man looks on the outward appearance, but the LORD looks on the heart" (1 Sam 16:7). The physical appearances of these dying people were at times distressing, naturally, but the hearts of many of the poor were so uplifting because they were so pure. As one volunteer put it, "You feel the presence of God there, and they feel the love. They die content." It was mostly their hearts that I noticed. That is why I thought it was such a beautiful place. As I worked, I felt that I was surrounded by angels, and I was ministering to angels.

Every day we looked straight into the eyes of those who were on the threshold of death. I spent an entire afternoon holding a poor woman who lay in her bed, pitifully gasping for each breath. She laid her head on my lap as I rubbed her back and held her hand. For two hours, I thought she was going to die any minute. It was amazing how she held on to life, clinging, gasping, and willing herself to stay alive.

I did not feel that I was doing things *to* these patients so much as I was doing things *with* them. We were experiencing things together. I truly felt as though I was seeing their hearts as much as their bodies. Touching their souls as much as their skeletal limbs. That is what made the work so meaningful. After the death of one young person, I felt that my gift to him was only a shadow of his gift to me as he looked up at me with his innocent eyes and young face. I thank God for the privilege of being able to lift at least part of his suffering. Every man whom I have touched and held in the Home for the Dying has passed away. They seem to go from my arms into the hands of God.

One morning nearing the end of my stay in Calcutta, I went to Mass at the Home for the Dying. I thoroughly enjoyed attending Mass, hearing the Gospel reading, and receiving Holy Communion while sitting alongside the suffering body of one of the dying destitutes. It was like being with Jesus in the most beautiful way. I had yet another one of my special men with me that day. I was immersed completely in caring for him the entire morning. I held and rubbed his hands and feet, and looked into his eyes, which registered deep contentment and intermittent agony. I rubbed his back as he vomited into the metal cup I had been holding for him throughout Mass. His sweet, gentle smile and nod of thanks just melted my heart. Before I left him, I could not resist embracing and kissing his feet, his thick-skinned, seemingly unfeeling, coarse feet which I had been massaging. I thought to myself that if I were to catch some random disease from him, it will still have been well worth the privilege of being with him.

Mother Teresa repeated, "In the Mass we have Jesus in the appearance of bread, while in the slums we touch Him in the broken bodies and in the abandoned children." Attending daily Mass and serving the dying each day made this the most spiritually nourishing experience I had ever had.

Photo courtesy of the Missionaries of Charity

The Poor Loved Mother Teresa

When Mother Teresa visited the Home for the Dying, all the patients who could lift their fragile arms would reach out to her. With childlike affection, they would call to her. She, more than anyone else, transformed the shelter into a place of joy.

No matter where she went, people loved her. I could com-

Calcutta's poor loved Mother Teresa as a mother. She, in turn, was most comfortable and at home with the poor, with children, with ordinary people, with the little ones of the world. She had a real affinity for those for whom our Savior had an affinity.

pletely relate to what Malcolm Muggeridge wrote in his book *Something Beautiful for God* about Mother Teresa: "When she is away in Europe or America, she only longs to be back in Calcutta with her poor. These are her beloved. Walking with her among them … I kept hearing the muttered word '*Mother!*' It wasn't that they had anything to say to her or to ask her; just that they wanted to establish contact with her, to know she was there. I quite understood."

Poverty Is Caused by Us

Only a lack of love is responsible for poverty. It is a result of our refusal to share with others.
MOTHER TERESA

"Poverty is not created by God, it's made by you and me. We are responsible [for it] because we don't share. Even God will not force us to do good. We must *choose* to do the good."[34]

Mother Teresa explained that the poor are "those whom society rejects and abandons. We try to give human dignity back to these people. As children of God they have a right to it." We cause interior poverty whenever we strip people of their dignity through neglect, indifference, and lack of love. We can restore human dignity through love and compassion, through genuine respect and understanding, humble service, and through firm believing that each person is truly "created in the image and likeness of God."

In Calcutta, poverty took on a human face for me every day. I remember the first time I helped to clean up a newcomer who had been brought in from the streets to the Home for the Dying on a stretcher. Her body was parched, dry, and dusty. All this poor woman had on when we took her in was a rough, dirty sackcloth wrapped around her skeletal body and a few simple bracelets dangling around her tiny wrists. A cloth and some bracelets. These were all her earthly belongings. It was such a striking contrast to all that we possess in our lives. As I was setting aside her bracelets and her canvas dress in order to bathe her, I could not help but think about all our possessions in the Western world, all the "stuff" that fills our homes, our closets, our offices, our shelves. In Calcutta, there was such stark and striking poverty, such total destitution. "The only thing that can remove poverty is sharing," Mother Teresa repeated. "Jesus came among the poorest to teach people to love one another, which is to share, to use the gifts that God has given to people who have, to share with those who have not."[35]

I was astounded by the poverty of the little ones in the Children's Home as well. For example, the poverty of a little girl crying while sitting on her small toilet. Since it was "potty time," I could not lift this little girl up at that moment to console her and dry her tears. I looked around the orphanage to find a toy or something that might make her happy. I could not see any toys. All I could find was a little piece of string. Since there was nothing else, I decided to give it a try. As soon as I placed it in her hands, she stopped crying. I was truly amazed. I have interacted with children in the United States for many years; I cannot imagine that a little piece of string would ever satisfy the cries of any of them. In fact, if I were to give them such an insignificant thing while they were upset, it would probably make them cry even louder! I discovered a striking contrast between those children in India and the little ones here in the more affluent countries. I saw some of the beautiful aspects of poverty, how it sometimes makes people very easy to please. The hearts of the poor seemed to be happy with very little.

We Are All Poor in One Way or Another

When Mother Teresa brought her Missionaries of Charity to the United States, people asked the Sisters: "Are you finished with India? What do you want to do here?" As one of the Sisters explained: "I think Mother knew better than anyone else that she also had a mission to New York, London, Rome … all these places." She continued, saying that when they came to New York "it was very difficult; their poverty was much deeper."

"There are many in the world dying for a piece of bread but many more dying for a little love," Mother Teresa said. "The poverty in the West is not only a poverty of loneliness, but also of spirituality. There is a hunger for love, as there is a hunger for God."[36]

"There are hungry people *everywhere*," she insisted. "But poverty is not just being without food. It is the absence of love. I can tell you there is more warmth in Calcutta, where people are willing to share

"Around the world, not only in the poor countries, I found the poverty of the West so much more difficult to remove. When I pick up a person from the street, hungry, I give him a plate of rice, a piece of bread, and I have satisfied that hunger. But a person that has been thrown out from society — that poverty is so hurtful and so much that I find it very difficult." Mother Teresa

what there is, than in many places where they have everything"[37] She often pointed this out, explaining it in different ways: "There are two kinds of poverty. We have the poverty of material things…. But there are also those who are poor in other ways … victims of a life that has stripped them of meaning, or a sense of being alive, or realizing their full potential by using the gifts that God gave them to love." This latter type of poverty is most pitiful of all. It was always clear that our kind of poverty here in the West was most troubling to Mother Teresa.

Mother Teresa Freely Chose to Be Poor

Mother Teresa did not live with modern conveniences and comforts. She voluntarily chose to live a most simple and humble lifestyle. In the documentary film *Mother Teresa*, Mother said: "Many people don't understand why we don't have washing machines, why we don't have fans, why we don't go to cinemas, why we don't go to parties. These are natural things and there's nothing wrong in having them.

But for us we have chosen *not* to have…. For us to be able to understand the poor, we must know what is poverty…."

Mother Teresa and each of her Sisters took a solemn vow of poverty, and they really live their vow to the hilt! In their houses, they have no carpeting, no fans, no televisions, no dishwashers, no vacuum cleaners, no privacy, no personal possessions except the most basic. They sacrifice everything. It is a beautiful sacrifice because it is complete. They have a total confidence in God's mercy, a complete trust in Divine Providence. "Divine Providence is always giving to us in ways most unexpected … it's such a delight to know that we don't really have to worry, no matter what we need and want for our people, it will be there. And even for ourselves, the way God provides for us is just fantastic!" Sister Priscilla said, and each of the Sisters could echo.

Mother Teresa, throughout most of her life, "identified herself with human suffering and privation," as one journalist wrote. I witnessed that she and the Sisters voluntarily ate what the poor had no choice but to eat every day. Their lifestyle was very rustic and unsophisticated. They traveled by foot much of the time. Their material possessions were astonishingly sparse: each Sister owned two saris (one to wash, one to wear), rosary beads, prayer books, and little else. Their saris were of the same simple cotton as those of the poor whom they served. "Whatever is given to the poor is the same for us," Mother Teresa said.

Money is helpful, without a doubt; but only love and understanding reach the heart and give peace and hope. Mother Teresa believed that poverty can only be cured by love. Medicine and material things can certainly alleviate some of the suffering, but it is the understanding love in our hearts that can heal the loneliness, despair, and rejection of the poor. All the money in the world cannot heal a heart.

"Seek and You Shall Find" the Littlest and the Least

Find them, love them, put your love for them into living action.
MOTHER TERESA

Sometimes we have to go searching for those in need of our mercy. Sometimes we have to go out of our way.

Crossing the very long and impressive Howrah Bridge, which spanned the Hooghly River and which connected the two massive "twin cities" of Calcutta and Howrah, and seeing what was on the other side, was an unforgettable experience. Under this bridge is one of the largest and indescribably desperate slums anywhere, like a black pit where multitudes of people live in absolute squalor. Mud, flies, mangy animals, and skeletal bodies all reside there together. Beyond this bridge, deep in the city of Howrah, is the orphanage run by Mother Teresa's missionaries.

This children's home was filled with sick, destitute little ones who just LOVED affection. The tiniest children here LOVED to be cuddled. In most cases, this was easy to do. In some cases, sadly enough, it was tough because it involved risk of contamination. For example, we were not supposed to hug the young boy covered with broken skin and scabies, which is a highly contagious, parasitical skin disease. These children seemed to have everything, from TB to dysentery to blister-like bumps all over their faces and bodies, to lice, to who-knows-what. There was one precious infant who clung to anyone who sympathetically lifted her up and held her. Her cry was almost silent, as if her little lungs couldn't do more. She was a cuddler! She was so thoroughly content just to be held and loved.

After just one day as a volunteer, I could see the difference love made — it showed in smiles on the children's faces.

Children Are a Blessing

The child is the beauty of God present in the world, the greatest gift to a family.
                                        MOTHER TERESA

When I consider Christ's words: "…as you did it to one of the least of these my brethren, you did it to me"(Mt 25:40), I think especially of the little ones in society, the children and the unborn. These truly are the most innocent, most defenseless and vulnerable, and most precious in God's sight. The Lord said: "Before I formed you in the womb I knew you, and before you were born I consecrated you" (Jer 1:5). Astonishingly, what we as a society do to these little ones, "the least" among us, we do directly to God. The Lord has so often shown a special preference for the little and least throughout all generations. The Scriptures tell us that David was chosen by the Lord to be king, even though he was the youngest brother. Bethlehem was chosen by God to be the birthplace of our Savior, even though it was a little town. In Deuteronomy, Chapter 7, the Lord tells His people in Israel that they are ". . . a people holy to the LORD your God …" not because they were the largest of nations, rather that He had "set his love upon them and chose them" because they were the *smallest* of nations (Deut 7:6-7). God has always loved the little ones.

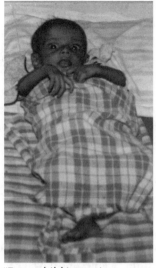

"Every child is precious, every child is a gift of God." Mother Teresa

Chapter Seven

❧

We Are All Called to Holiness

You shall be holy; for I the LORD your God am holy.
LEVITICUS 19:2

"Holiness Is Not the Luxury of a Few...."

Mother Teresa told us that sanctity is within reach of every heart and it should not be rare. This was one of her greatest lessons, I believe. "Holiness is not just for a few people," she said. "It's for everyone, including you." To Mother Teresa, holiness was not just an ideal; it was a responsibility. Jesus Himself called us to "...be perfect, as your heavenly Father is perfect" (Mt 5:48), and Mother Teresa so often echoed Christ's teachings. "So let us be holy as our Father in heaven is holy," she said. Since this is the vocation of each of us, it is good to understand exactly what this entails.

The saints give us beautiful definitions of holiness, but it is especially the example of their lives that teaches us what holiness is and what we are called to be:

"Holiness consists in doing God's Will joyfully. Faithfulness makes saints. The first step toward holiness is the will to become holy. Through a firm and upright will, we love God, we choose God, we hasten to God, we reach Him, we have Him." [38]

"Holiness does not consist in doing extraordinary things. It consists in accepting, with a smile, what Jesus sends us."[39]

"Sanctity is a disposition of the heart which makes us humble and little in the arms of God, aware of our weakness and

155

confident even unto audacity in the goodness of our heavenly Father."[40]

"Nothing can make us holy except the presence of God … and to me the presence of God is in fidelity to little things."[41]

Mother Teresa taught us that simple human thoughtfulness is the beginning of holiness. "If you learn the art of being thoughtful, you will be more and more like Christ; His heart was kind and gentle, and He always thought of others. Jesus did good wherever He went." We must be like that too.

She continued: "The quickest and surest way [toward thoughtfulness] is the 'tongue' — use it for the good of others. If you think well of others, you will also speak well of others and to others. 'From the abundance of the heart the mouth speaketh.' If your heart is full of love, you will speak of love. Violence of the tongue is very real — sharper than any knife, wounding and creating bitterness that only the grace of God can heal."[42]

Words are indeed powerful. They can bring great sadness and destruction, or they can cause joy and create peace. It is up to us to choose.

Are You a Light in the World?

"If you are already a saint, thank God. If you are a sinner, don't remain one," Mother Teresa advised. And she taught us *how* to be saints in so many ways. Her words and ways were always simple and practical. "Be kind and merciful. Let no one ever come to you without leaving better and happier." "Be the living expression of God's kindness — kindness in your face, kindness in your eyes, kindness in your smile, kindness in your warm greeting."

"Make every effort to walk in the presence of God, to see God in everyone you meet," Mother Teresa taught. "You should always be praying with all your heart and soul."

In the book *Something Beautiful for God* Mother said: "We must become holy, not because we want to *feel* holy but because Christ must be able to live His life fully in us. We are to be all love, all faith, all purity…. And once we have learned to seek God and His will, our contacts with the poor will become the means of great sanctity to our-selves and to others."

Whether we realize it or not, we are having an influence on other lives simply by the way we are living our own. Our deeds of darkness contaminate the minds and lives of others, while our righteous acts of love may inspire and uplift the minds and ways of others. What kind of example we are setting? If only we would really take to heart these words of Bishop Oscar Romero, the slain archbishop of El Salvador: "Be careful of what you say and do, for you may be the only Bible some people will ever read."

While sin spreads darkness, holiness and goodness bring light. Mother Teresa taught us to be a bright light in the world by being near to God. Before I met her, I was very touched by these simple words she had written:

> Often you see small and big wires, new and old, cheap and expensive electric cables up — they alone are useless and until the current passes through them, there will be no light. The wire is you and me. The current is God. We have the power to let the current pass through us and use us to produce the light of the world or we can refuse to be used and allow the darkness to spread. My prayer is with each one of you and I pray that each one of you will be *holy*, and so spread God's love everywhere you go. Let His light of truth be in every person's life so that God can continue loving the world through you and me. Put your heart into being a bright light.[43]

These words explain how Mother Teresa's life was a bright light in the world. She was so connected to the source of all life, all holiness, and all love. Her union with God brought forth the fruit of sanctity. It was what made standing in her presence like a taste of heaven on earth. It is powerful to remember that we are like wires, and we have it within our ability to let the light of God shine through everything we do.

A reporter in the film *Mother Teresa* said to Mother: "Some people feel that you are almost like a living saint. How do you feel about that?" Mother, in her direct and simple manner, responded so beautifully: "You have to be holy in your position as you are, and I have to be holy in the position that God has put me. So it is nothing extraordinary to be holy. Holiness is not the luxury of the few. Holiness is a simple duty for you and for me. We have been created for that."

Mother Teresa quoted Saint Thomas as saying: "'Sanctity consists in nothing else but a firm resolve,' the heroic act of a soul abandoning itself to God." And she herself added, in a letter written to me in May of 1997: "…our progress in holiness depends on God and on ourselves, on God's grace and on our will to be holy. We must have a real living determination to reach holiness. Let us ask Our Lady to help us to keep our hearts pure so that we can love Christ, her Son, with tenderness and love…."

Love, perhaps more than anything else, is what makes us holy. It makes us like God, Who is love. Saint Thérèse said: "Great love, not great deeds, is the essence of sanctity." Guide us, dear God, and grant us a *real* holiness, a *deep* holiness, a *lasting* holiness, like the kind of holiness that we witnessed in Mother Teresa. Not a shallow kind that changes with the world and seeks to appeal to the world instead of seeking to please *You* Who are the same yesterday, today, and for all eternity. Mother wanted each of us to be holy, and to "Let His light of truth be in every person's life, so that God can continue loving the world through you and me." She wrote: "Keep giving Jesus to others, not by words, but by your example … by radiating His holiness and spreading His fragrance of love everywhere you go. Just keep the joy of Jesus as your strength. Be happy and at peace."

I believe that one of the most beautiful things about Mother's holy ways is that they were not inimitable. "Love is a fruit in season at all times and within the reach of every hand," she said. "Anyone may gather it and no limit is set. Everyone can reach this love through meditation, spirit of prayer, and sacrifice, by an intense inner life." Holiness, love, and compassion should be as natural as living and breathing.

I think that Mother Teresa's saintly nature is within reach of us all. We are all undoubtedly able to become saints, but we must be willing to grow, to sacrifice, to suffer, and to love. We are like seeds. Mother Teresa was a flower in full bloom because she had "died" to herself just as a seed must fall to the ground and die in order that new life may spring forth.

Mother Teresa revealed to us our own potential as human beings. She was walking, breathing, living proof that we can become holy, that we can become like Christ. However, there is a price to pay. We must be willing to care for ourselves, to care about our spiritual well-being, nourishment, and growth. We must be willing to weed out our bad qualities and tendencies, to aim high, to grow ever onward and upward, to strive always to become more open, better individuals, more like Jesus Himself.

"Christians are light for each other and for the rest of the world," Mother Teresa said. "If we are Christians, we have to reveal Christ. Gandhi once said that if Christians truly lived their Christianity, there would be no Hindus in India. This, therefore, is what everyone expects from us: that our Christianity be real." Mother Teresa encouraged us all to "keep the light of Christ always burning in your heart."

Mother Teresa wanted very much for people to, "Come to know God, to love Him, to serve Him, for that is true happiness. And what I have I want everyone in the world to have. But it is their choice. If they have seen the light they can follow it. I cannot give them the light: I can only give the means."

True happiness, peace, love, and holiness all go hand-in-hand, even if they are also accompanied by true suffering. Our trials are, in fact, a means to greater sanctity and deeper joy.

"Suffering Is a Gift of God"

Sorrow both cleanses the soul and makes peace with God.
SAINT THOMAS À KEMPIS

I learned as a young child that life on earth is a journey through "the valley of tears." It is a pilgrimage to heaven. It was not meant to be easy, and it is only natural that suffering should come during this earthly exile. Only in the "Promised Land" of heaven would our souls find true happiness and endless peace. This is why I was always amazed and thoroughly delighted at each of life's blessings and joys, at all the sweet and good things in life, because I was not expecting them in such abundance during this time of exile. "When one expects pure and unmixed suffering, the smallest joy becomes an un-hoped for surprise," Saint

Thérèse of Lisieux once wrote. My journey through Calcutta was like my journey through life. When one is expecting a "valley of tears" and instead one experiences so much spiritual joy, one cannot help but raise one's eyes to heaven with boundless gratitude and a smile.

Clearly, there is great purifying and redemptive value in suffering. I would never ask for it personally, but when it comes, it is good to see it in a new way, to embrace it willingly and let God do great things with it. Let it humble our hearts, sanctify our souls, fill us with compassion for others who suffer. Let it test our faith and strengthen our love "like gold tested in fire." If only we would learn to draw profit from the good as well as the bad in our lives, from the sunshine as well as the rain, and realize that everything that happens to us can serve to make us become better than before, with the help of God's grace. Pain, humiliation, sickness, and failure, Mother Teresa said, "are a gift of God, a gift that makes us most Christ-like. People must not accept suffering as a punishment."

Photo by Paul Hulewicz

Mother Teresa said: "Anyone who imitates Jesus to the full must also share in His Passion. We must have the courage to pray, have the courage to accept. Because we do not pray enough, we see only the human part. We don't see the divine. And we resent it…. Suffering is meant to purify, to sanctify, to make us Christ-like."[44] Mother Teresa, giving of herself to everyone, with grace and love.

Rich and poor alike have to endure hardship on this earth in one form or another. There are many rich people who must suffer loneliness, annoyances, solitude, being prisoners of money, illness, unhappy marriages, and so on. Suffering can serve, spiritually, as one of our greatest blessings. Saint Francis de Sales said it is made much more effective "by a pure, simple acceptance of God's will." If we can learn to look at suffering in positive light, and learn to embrace it rather than shun it when it comes to us, we will have found a great secret of happiness.

During a personal experience of tremendous loneliness and what one might call "the dark night of the soul," I received a very enlightening and uplifting letter from a wonderful friend, Father Conrad De Meester of Belgium. Reading his words, I discovered how powerful and comforting it is to remember, whenever we cannot see "the light at the end of the tunnel," that *Jesus is in the tunnel too*! God is *with* us. This simple realization can change suffering into unspeakable joy. It can easily change our darkness into light. My friend also reminded me that what suffering excavates in our souls, a deeper joy and peace can then fill in. It is amazing what a difference it makes when we change our way of looking at things. "We should not rest in useless looks at our own miseries," Mother Teresa said, "but should lift our hearts to God and His light."

I believe the patients in the Home for the Dying found comfort and peace because they were not alone. God was with them and we were with one another. Mother Teresa explained it beautifully: "Suffering, if it is accepted together, borne together, is joy." For those who were in pain and experiencing tremendous difficulties, Mother gave comfort by reminding them that there was great reason to hope. She would say: "Remember that the Passion of Christ ends always in the joy of the Resurrection of Christ, so when you feel in your own heart the suffering of Christ, remember the resurrection has to come, the joy of Easter has to dawn. Never let anything so fill you with sorrow as to make you forget the joy of the risen Christ."

The way to heaven and eternal beatitude has always been the way of the Cross. Suffering with faith-filled surrender and love has always been a path to holiness, and it is one of the most perfect ways to save other souls, too. To make it all the way, we need strength and grace. We need prayer. We need God. We need to take it one day at a time. The present moment is never intolerable. It is most often our worry about the future that causes the greatest suffering. We are taught by Jesus to concern ourselves only with today, for tomorrow has enough cares of its own (Mt 6:25). Jesus beckons us to stop worrying and to trust God. The way that God chooses for us is the way that He knows is *best* for our salvation.

"Do not look forward to what may happen tomorrow; the same everlasting God who cares for you today will take care of you tomorrow, and every day," Saint Francis de Sales said. "Either God will shield you from suffering, or God will give you unfailing strength to bear it."

I have learned to view suffering not only as a *reality* for each individual in this life, but also, through Mother Teresa's teachings, as a sign of God's love. In Scripture it says: "for the LORD reproves him whom he loves, as a father the son in whom he delights" (Prov 3:12). This is

"Many are the afflictions of the righteous; but the LORD delivers him out of them all" (Ps 34:20). So many of the saints remind us that suffering is very profitable to our souls, troublesome and grievous though it may be, for in it we are humbled, purified, and instructed. All the saints passed through many sufferings. That, and not a comfortable life, is what made them saints. In the words of Saint Thérèse, considered one of the greatest saints of modern times: "Trials help greatly to detach us from earth. They make us look to God, rather than to this world."

the way God has always treated His beloved children, with discipline. Even His *only begotten Son*, Our Lord and Savior Jesus, while on earth was a man of sorrows. Indeed, Christ came not to live an easy life, but to suffer for love of us and for the salvation of our souls. We are called to imitate Christ: to pick up our cross and follow Him. He accepted suffering and death, and through His suffering He won for us eternal happiness. It is important to see the bright side of suffering because, in some form or another, we all have to bear it in our lives.

Mother Teresa not only witnessed tremendous human suffering every day for most of her long life, but she also endured much personal hardship, and yet she never lost her spirit of faith, her radiance of joy, or the warmth of love. Looking at her was a beautiful lesson in holiness.

My First Impressions of Mother Teresa Were Lasting Ones

Talking with her was a constant delight.
MALCOLM MUGGERIDGE

The very first day I laid eyes on Mother Teresa was August 6, the Feast of the Transfiguration of Jesus. This was an interesting coincidence, since my personal goals in life underwent a radical "transfiguration" after meeting Mother Teresa. This feast commemorates the time when Our Lord brought three of His disciples up onto a mountain to pray; while He was with them, Jesus suddenly became radiant and resplendent in glory. Scripture tells us "…as he was praying, the appearance of his countenance was altered, and his raiment became dazzling white" (Lk 9:29). Suddenly Moses and Elijah appeared too, and they were speaking with Jesus. Saint Peter, one of the disciples who witnessed this, exclaimed: "Master, how good it is for us to be here!" This remark was the understatement of all time! I could have exclaimed the same thing on the day that I met Mother Teresa. The sight of her was glorious to me and I felt so totally blessed to have been standing in her presence. How good it was to have been there and to have beheld this living saint. It was certainly one of the great "mountaintop experiences" of my life. Mother Teresa was 75 years old when I met her for the first time; I had just turned 21, and my heart was very sensitive, open, eager to learn, and so eager to love. She was so beautiful to me!

On the day I first met Mother Teresa, I had gone to the Mother-house for morning Mass and had gone up the stairs to the chapel. It was filled with the Sisters in their white saris. I genuflected and went to my usual spot. Mother Teresa happened to be kneeling to the left of me, less than a hop, skip, and jump away! I knelt and concentrated on saying my morning prayers. As Mass started, other volunteers piled into the chapel, and a couple of women crowded in between Mother Teresa and me. I was thankful to have had my special time alone with her and the Sisters.

During Holy Communion, I received the Body of Christ from Mother Teresa's hands. It was one of the most touching, penetrating, all-encompassing, beautiful realizations of my entire life. I was over-whelmed in a wonderful way. When I returned to my place on the floor after receiving Holy Communion, I knelt down, bowed down to the ground, and wept, showering the crucifix on my rosary beads in my hands with tears. I was awed by the awareness of what I had just experienced. And I thanked God with all my heart.

Mother Teresa left the chapel before I did. I stayed until the very last of the novices finished their after-Mass prayers, and so did not get a chance to speak with her.

During my first encounters with Mother Teresa, as she spoke to a small group of us or as she knelt on the floor in prayer, I was struck by her profound humility. I knew that she was world famous and I had imagined that all famous people have a sense of their own greatness, a pride that shows through in their words and manners. There was none of that in Mother Teresa. There was an apparent selflessness in her, a quality that is not easy to find, even in non-famous people. It was as if she was totally unaware of herself, as if she was aware of only God and others. I had never met anyone in my life as humble as Mother Teresa. She was as humble as the poor whom we would lift up out of the gutters. Her humility was strikingly beautiful to me.

Mother Teresa embodied so many other qualities as well, qualities that are all too rare in the world today. I wished that I could have brought her home with me, shown her to everyone, and said: "Just look at her!" Her appearance, her spirit, and her *presence* spoke a thou-sand words about integrity, about God, about true beauty, about inner strength, about love. Before meeting her, I had held incredibly high expectations and hopes concerning her, and I was not disappointed in the least. The reality was even better than what I had imagined. All that I learned about her and from her had been true-to-life. I have no doubt in my mind that Mother Teresa is truly a saint.

I would have thought that faith, love, joy, and humility were invisible things, but as I stood and watched Mother, I could see what true joy was. I could see it shining from her face. I could see what love was. It emanated from her whole being! I could see humility as if it were something tangible. For the first time in my life, I understood why artists tend to depict saints as having halos. There was something shining through Mother Teresa, something you could see. For those around her, her humility strengthened our faith, enlivened our love, deepened our own humility, and made our joy impossible to contain.

It seemed to me that most volunteers were a little bit hesitant to go and visit with her. After all, what could one say of importance to Mother Teresa? But my love for her was much stronger than fear. I had a great longing to be near her. And what a wonderful difference this made, for my visits with Mother Teresa added great richness and joy to my experience. They are treasures that I will always cherish.

Each contact with Mother, every glimpse of her, and all the words I heard her speak had profound repercussions in my soul. I remember most of my encounters with her as if they happened only yesterday. On the evening of that first day, I was able to see her a second time. Following Adoration, the volunteers congregated in the visitors' room of the Motherhouse. Mother Teresa came and stood right beside me as she spoke to our little gathering about praying and loving the least of our brothers and sisters. She told us that it was very valuable and good to love and serve the poorest, the loneliest, the most suffering, the least of our brethren, because Our Lord Jesus said that when we do this, we do it to Christ Himself. "You did it to Me," she said, recalling Christ's words. Then she reached over and took my right hand and said those same words, touching each one of my five fingers. After she finished, I held out my hand again, because I was so happy that Mother Teresa had been holding my hand in *her* blessed hands to teach a lesson. Seeing my outstretched hand, she must have thought that I was confused about what she was saying, because she repeated this gesture a few more times, using me to demonstrate her kept putting my hand out for her to take, and she just t!

lcutta progressively got better and better, until I honest-ly could not believe that it was real. Mother Teresa remained with us throughout the rest of the summer. She was the most radiant, holy, humble, and awe-inspiring human being I have ever met. She was a living example of Christ's love in action. Being in her presence made you feel as if you were a little child, meek and humbled. She was wonderful! The entire month of August was something special. I was able to see Mother Teresa at least twice a day and I had beautiful opportunities to speak with her, one-to-one. When she asked me to do a personal favor for her, to make special drawings, I felt so honored and I was more than willing. I felt like I was on a special mission from God!

One reason my first impressions of Mother Teresa were enduring ones is that there was never any disguise. I found her to be so unchanging, so real. Her humility never left her, her warmth never disappeared, and her wonderful blend of humor and seriousness was a constant. She continued to show thoughtfulness throughout the time that I was with her, whether it was in Calcutta or in New York. Nothing was feigned. She did not put on airs. She did not try to impress anyone. She, like so many of the Missionaries of Charity, could be described as simple and transparent. In a world where there is so much superficiality and deception, she stood out in sharp contrast. Mother Teresa was genuinely humble, genuinely faithful, genuinely hap-

Photo by Rik Daze

Jesus is Pleased to Come to Us!!
As the TRUTH to be Told!!
And the LIFE to be Lived!!
As the LIGHT to be Lighted!!
And the LOVE to be Loved!!
As the JOY to be Given!!
And the PEACE to be Spread!!

MOTHER TERESA

One day, with a playful smile, she gave each of us her "business card."

py, and genuinely holy. Her niece said that "there are no shadows about her, and she deeply believes in what she thinks and what she does." To me, the mere sight of Mother Teresa was impressive and inspiring.

Truly, the light I saw in Calcutta was greater than any darkness there, for Mother Teresa was in this place. Although she lived in the world, she was "altogether unworldly," and this made her a light that dispelled darkness. If she had not been there doing what she was doing and spreading "the sunshine of God's love" in the black holes of the slums where there was so much human suffering, the whole world would have been much darker. She brought nothing less than the light of Christ, the light of truth, which shined through her.

As Mother Teresa was kneeling on the chapel floor, her head bent in prayer, one could actually see the intense radiance of love as she spent time with God. I sensed that being near her was like experiencing what it is like to stand in the presence of Christ. She embodied so many Christian virtues: humility, faith, mercy, wisdom, patience, kindness, love. She *exemplified* these virtues. Because of the way she treated each person — her warmth, empathy, the sparkle in her eyes — and because of her love for God and her favor with God, people of all faiths would come to her for a blessing. And she would take time to welcome and accept each one with care and respect. Whenever I spoke with Mother Teresa, I felt that my soul was laid bare before her, that she could see everything in my heart. Whenever I spoke with her, I was always completely open and honest.

She had a very direct way of speaking that was stunning. "What are you going to do [with your life]?" she asked my friend Paul as he was preparing to leave Calcutta and return to Sweden. The question, together with her deeply penetrating look, her warmth, and her intense seriousness, took us all totally by surprise. It was such an important question, and yet Paul and the rest of us were not prepared to answer it. She left us searching our hearts, pondering our futures, in light of her words.

Her answers often took many people by surprise, too. One time while I was with Mother Teresa in New York, I asked her: "Isn't Calcutta a beautiful place?" and she responded without any hesitation, with a twinkle in her eyes: "Yes! And I hope to see you there again someday," and grasping the folds of her sari, she added, "wearing one of *these*!"

Mother Teresa was so small in stature and humble of heart that she was both physically and spiritually able to reach the poor and sick people who gathered along her path. I loved to watch this. She would stop and bless each one and she brought so many smiles with her tender touch. I cannot express fully what love poured out of us all as we watched Mother. And everyone who saw her, even from a distance, was as touched as the people upon whom she rested her hands. It was like watching Jesus touch and heal those who were blind and sick. Mother Teresa's

Sometimes I would visit with Mother Teresa on the little wooden bench outside her office at the Motherhouse. These were such joyous occasions for me! It always felt like I was dreaming! It seemed too wonderful to be true.

touch seemed to heal people's hearts of any sadness. Her presence instantly brought sunshine. Everywhere she went, she transformed sadness into joy, despair into hope, suffering into a sense of being privileged to suffer.

When I came home from India, people would often ask me: "What is Mother Teresa like?" It was always a challenge to answer with mere words. I wished that I could simply say: "Come and see!" Come and *experience* what it was like to stand in her presence. It was beyond words. I can only repeat that you could truly see the radiance of love in her. It would shine through her and touch everyone around her. The best way I could describe Mother Teresa and the light shining through her was with this prayer, which I learned from her in Calcutta and which she prayed daily. It is called "Radiating Christ," and it beautifully captures the spirit of Mother Teresa and all the love and joy we felt whenever we were in her presence. She prayed this every day after receiving the Body of Christ in Holy Communion:

Dearest Jesus, help us to spread Your fragrance everywhere we go. Flood our souls with Your Spirit and Life. Penetrate and possess our whole being, so utterly, that our lives may only be a radiance of Yours. Shine through us, and be so in us that every soul we come in contact with may feel Your Presence in our soul. Let them look up and see no longer us, but only Jesus! Stay with us, and then we shall begin to shine as You shine, so to shine as to be a light to others. The light, Oh Jesus, will be all from You; none of it will be ours. It will be You, shining on others through us. Let us thus praise You in the way You love best: by shining on those around us. Let us preach You without preaching — not by words, but by our example, by the catching force, the sympathetic influence of what we do, and the evident fullness of the love our hearts bear to You. Amen.

"I think if we can spread this prayer, if we can translate it into our lives, it will make all the difference," Mother Teresa said. "It is so full of Jesus. It has made a great difference in the lives of the Missionaries of Charity."

Similar to what I experienced with the dying, except to a far greater degree, I did not notice the physical appearance in Mother Teresa so much as I noticed her spiritual presence. I kept referring to her as "beautiful!" I never noticed her wrinkles, or her small stature, or even the color of her eyes when I was with her. I was overwhelmed by the greatness and beauty of her spirit. There were occasions when, after having visited with her, I would go back out onto the streets of Calcutta and could not remember whether she had touched my hand or my shoulder as we spoke. It was

Although it is said that she was only about 4 feet 11 inches tall, it was not actually Mother Teresa's small stature that I noticed first. Rather, it was her unawareness of herself that touched me. She was strikingly humble.

as if she was too ethereal to be remembered vividly in a physical sense. But I could always remember the *feeling* of being in her presence. I could remember the wonderful swirling sense of awe, love, admiration, and excitement in my heart as I listened to her. Once when I was visiting with her she was called away for a few moments, and as she was leaving my side, I suddenly spilled out my feelings about her. I exclaimed: "I *love* you, Mother!" The sense of joy was the most remarkable. I could not hide it. I could not wipe the smile off my face.

I do remember a few things about her physical attributes: I noticed that her hands were soft, worn, strong, loving, prayerful, and holy. As I knelt close to her in the chapel, I also could not help noticing that her feet were unique: they were badly twisted and deformed from years of wearing ill-fitting sandals. Mother Teresa's singing voice was also distinguishable. There was no mistaking Mother's voice, which seemed to be a unique blend of various accents.

Humility

The nature of love is to humble oneself.
SAINT THÉRÈSE

One of the reasons why I love and admire Mother Teresa so much is that her humility was exemplary. This, to me, is a sign of true holiness. Humility is also one of the virtues in Our Lord Jesus that I love the most. The fact that the Son of God, Who could have remained in His glorious high heavens, humbled Himself to share in our humanity simply astounds me. The Master of us all has the most humble heart of all. God Almighty is more humble than we mere creatures are! Mother Teresa seemed to love and appreciate humility, too. "It is beautiful to see the humility of Christ," she said. "In God I find two things admirable: His goodness and His humility. His love and His humility are striking. God is truly humble; He comes down and uses instruments as weak and imperfect as we are. He deigns to work through us. Is that not marvelous?"

Mother Teresa wrote and spoke often about humility. "We must be humble, like God," she taught. This virtue is one of the essential ingredients of holiness and of closeness to God. "The more we empty ourselves, the more room we give God to fill us," she used to say. The more we forget ourselves, the more God will think of us. The more we detach ourselves from self, the more attached God will be to us. "…it is not how much we really 'have' to give, but how empty we are, so that we can receive fully in our life and let Him live His life in us."

Mother Teresa did not esteem herself better than others. She was very little in her own eyes. "I am nothing," she said. "He is all. I do nothing on my own. He does it. That is what I am: God's pencil…. However imperfect instruments we may be, He writes beautifully." Her littleness was truly her greatness. When she was awarded honors in recognition of her works of love and peace, which happened very often, she always felt that she did nothing to deserve them. She was never puffed up with pride or self-satisfaction. It was, after all, "God's work" that she was doing, as she was fond of saying. She so often referred to herself not only as a pencil, but as a "*little* pencil" in God's Hand. She realized that all our talents and achievements are God's gifts to us. He is the one who deserves all the credit. "If it was not for God's tender love, every moment of the day, we would be nothing," she said.

Mother Teresa received the world's highest accolades while remaining grounded in humility; she continued to seek out the poor, the dying,

Mother Teresa in the women's section of the Home for the Dying, speaking with Sister Luke. I loved to watch her shine her love onto the patients in this place of the pure heart.

and the unloved; she continued to love others in a lowly, simple and earnest way.

"We must not drift away from the humble works," she insisted, "because these are the works nobody will do. It is never too small. We are so small we look at things in a small way. But God, being Almighty, sees everything great. Therefore, even if you write a letter for a blind man or you just go and sit and listen, or you take in the mail for him, or you visit somebody or bring a flower to somebody, small things, or wash clothes for somebody or clean the house. Very humble work that is where you and I must be. For there are many people who can do big things. But there are very few people who will do the small things" (*LOVE: A Fruit Always in Season*).

"Knowledge of God gives love, and knowledge of self gives humility," she said. "Humility is nothing but truth. 'What have we got that we have not received?' asks Saint Paul. 'If I have received everything, what good have I of my own?' If we are convinced of this, we will never raise our head in pride. If you are humble, nothing will touch you, neither praise nor disgrace, because you know what you are…. Self-knowledge puts us on our knees."[45]

Mother Teresa Was a Living Prayer

A good person is a prayer.
SAINT CATHERINE OF SIENA

For many years, Mother Teresa was known throughout the world as "a living saint." I always called her a *living prayer*, for she did not just *say* her prayers, she *lived* them. She *embodied* them. A beautiful example of this is the "Prayer for Peace," which she prayed every day. "Lord, make me a channel of Your peace. Where there is hatred, let me bring Your love…." Mother Teresa did not just say these words with her lips. This was her life. Where there was despair in life, she brought hope. Where there was sadness, she brought joy. Where there was darkness, she brought light. Where there was doubt, she brought true faith. Mother often used the word "beautiful" to describe things. Everything was beautiful to her. And when I came home from India, I found myself using that very word to describe her.

Mother Teresa was a living image of God's compassion, tenderness, humility, and goodness to me. She was an embodiment of God's mercy upon His beloved poor. I had written in my photo album, beneath a photograph of Mother Teresa in the Home for the Dying, that she was "one of the holiest, most revered, honored, respected, and dearly loved people in my life."

Not only was she a living prayer, but being with her was the answer to my prayer. Mother Teresa's soul was golden, brilliant, deeply penetrating and inspiring, very lovable, humble, approachable, pure, and simple. She was truly a shining example for the whole human race. God had blessed me exceedingly well in giving me an opportunity to see this holy person whom I had admired for so long and in whose presence I had yearned to be. I had never dreamed that I would be able to actually speak with her, to hear her words of wisdom and of truth and of God, to receive her blessings and prayers for a holy marriage and for my beloved family, to see her at least twice a day, to kneel at her side in the chapel, to be touched by her — both physically and spiritually — to do her wonderful work (which was a more beautiful privilege than I ever imagined it would be), to stand in her presence and serve God with her, to create drawings and paintings at her request and with her instructions, to express my feelings of love and gratitude toward her, to witness her radiance and her living love of Christ. She was a shining star, which I would follow through life, just as the three kings followed the star that led them to Christ.

I could never thank God enough for Mother Teresa, but I will always keep trying. I love her. I think of her when I say the divine praises, ending with "Blessed be God in His angels and in His saints!"

How Do We Know What God Is Calling Us to Do?

Wherever God has put you, that is your vocation.
MOTHER TERESA

This one small person has touched the lives of millions of people throughout the world, and even after her passing, she continues to touch lives. It is tremendously profitable and inspiring, I believe, to look closely at how Mother Teresa discerned the will of God in her life and remained faithful to His divine inspirations. In the book *Faith and Compassion: The Life and Work of Mother Teresa*, her spiritual adviser said (surprisingly!): "Mother Teresa was not an exceptional person. She was ... a very ordinary person, but with great love for her Lord...." If we, likewise, can imitate her love of the Lord and learn to totally surrender ourselves to His holy will as she did, we may see wonders and marvels in the unfolding of our own lives as well. Even though we might be ordinary souls, we may be able to say with her: ". . . he who is mighty has done great things for me" (Lk 1:49).

When Mother Teresa was young, a priest named Father Jambrenkovic taught her "the call of God would invariably be accompanied by deep joy." To follow one's heart and one's joy is to follow God's will. "At eighteen, I decided to leave home to become a nun," Mother Teresa said. "By then I realized that my vocation was towards the poor. From then on, I have never had the least doubt of my decision." Pointing a finger heavenward, she added: "It was the will of God. He made the choice."[46]

Mother Teresa's first "call" from God was to serve the poor. This is what led her to the Loreto Sisters with whom she lived and taught at an all-girls' school in Calcutta; but there was a further call, a very distinct, mysterious, and life-giving one. Her belonging to Christ would not change, but everything else would. Her spiritual director said: "It was not a vision [which led her out of the convent and into the slums of Calcutta], it was a communication that came as a form of inspiration. She felt distinctly that she had to leave Loreto and start her own work. She has never doubted, not for a moment," said Father Van Exem, Mother Teresa's long-time spiritual adviser. He added that it was a "real vocation, a real call, and subsequently all that has happened is difficult to explain in a natural way."[47]

Prayer is necessary in discerning one's vocation, as is an earnest *desire* to know God's will. The lives of the saints show us that if we cooperate with divine inspirations and the guidance offered to us by God, our lives will far surpass, in beauty and in fruitfulness, our own plans and even our wildest dreams.

September 10, 1946 was the day when Mother received her "call within a call" to leave the Loreto convent and go to work in the slums with the Poorest of the Poor. It was such an important date that it continues to be celebrated by the Missionaries of Charity as "Inspiration Day." This date marks the spiritual conception of the Missionaries of Charity. "The message was quite clear," Mother Teresa said. "It was an order. I was to leave the convent. I felt God wanted something more from me. He wanted me to be poor and to love Him in the distressing disguise of the Poorest of the Poor." She needed to practice the virtue of total confidence in God. "I knew where I belonged, but I did not know how to get there."[48]

Mother Teresa said, "All of us have been called.... The fact that you have been given a gift may constitute a call," since gifts are meant to be shared. Mother Teresa also pointed out that love is more important than the nature of our gifts and services: "So for all of us, it doesn't matter what we do or where we are as long as we remember that we belong to Him, that we are His, that we are in love with Him. The means He gives us, whether we are working for the rich or we are working for the poor, whether we are working with high-class people or low-class people ... makes no difference; but how much love we are putting into the work we do is what matters."[49] Her namesake, Saint Thérèse, likewise affirmed: "I know that LOVE strengthens every vocation, that love is everything, that it embraces all times and all places, because it is eternal." Love is one of the most important elements in discovering God's will, because it is at the very heart of God's will for each one of us. Love is the fulfillment of God's plan for our lives.

Having an open heart is another key element in the process of knowing God's will. When I visited Mother Teresa's convent in New York as a "come and see" for two weeks, at her request, she told me to make sure that I was leaving the door to my heart totally open. I smiled and told her that not only would I leave the door to my heart open, but I would take the door off its hinges. There would be no door at all! It is so important to openly consider all options and possibilities, "For as the heavens are higher than the earth" so high are God's ways above our ways (Is 55:9). Unless we are totally open to anything, we may be missing the greatest possibilities of our lives.

When one's heart is set on fulfilling God's will, one has every reason to be happy. Father Conrad De Meester once wrote to me: "Be happy, dear Susan, because your main suffering concerns knowing His will.... So, if you don't arrive at certitude about His will, about His very concrete will, know that it is His will that you *don't* know His will, and know that you are living His will in the darkness [of faith]. One day, light will shine without limits!" It is so important for us to love God even in the darkness. Even when we do not see what He wants of us, we can be filled with confidence and love. As Thérèse herself said: "One day you will be happy to have suffered" for such a beautiful cause.

While we were together in Calcutta, Mother Teresa asked me, "What are you going to do?" It was my moment of truth. I answered her simply and as honestly as I knew how, looking straight into her deep, penetrating, radiant eyes. I knew that she was asking what I was planning to do with my life and I answered her: "I am going to follow my heart each step of the way, as I did in coming to Calcutta...." Apparently this was not good enough, because she pressed on. She asked me what made me happier: the thought of marriage or the thought of the religious life. This led to a whole conversation about the dreams of marriage that I had always cherished since I was a little girl.

I told her that the thought of the married life filled me with much peace, love, and joy; that my upbringing in a large, strong, loving, and faithful family made me want to have a holy and faithful family of my own. She seemed to accept my heartfelt answer and she immediately went on from there: "Do you know who he is?" That is, did I know who my future husband would be? I answered that I was not sure, I did not know. I revealed to Mother Teresa that ever since I was a young girl I would pray to the Blessed Mother to somehow bring a wonderful man like Saint Joseph into my life. Mother said that she would pray for a saint-like, good man for me to marry. She would pray for me to have a holy marriage. I was *beyond* being overjoyed. I could not believe what I was hearing! Mother Teresa not only approved of my choosing the path of marriage and didn't place any pressure on me to enter the religious life, but she said that she would *pray* for me to find that special someone and to have a holy marriage. I had received Mother Teresa's blessings! She couldn't have pleased me more than she did that day.

My diary, August 26: *When Mother Teresa gave me her blessing and God's blessing for a holy marriage and for my beloved family at home, it was beyond what I had dreamed! She also told me to pray to the Blessed Mother (and to a saint whose name I unfortu-*

nately cannot recall) not only about finding a special spouse, but
also about there being a member of the family to enter the reli-
gious life, which is a blessing, she feels.

One more thing I learned about God's ways of leading souls is that
He is full of surprises. Saint Paul said: "...no eye has seen, nor ear
heard, nor the heart of man conceived, what God has prepared for
those who love him" (1Cor 2:9). What I am doing with my life today,
I never could have imagined five years ago. It simply never crossed my
mind. That is why it is good to make plans, certainly, but it is also
important to remain open to any possibility that has not yet dawned
on us. The best practice is to "Trust in the LORD with all your heart,
and do not rely on your own insight. In all your ways acknowledge
him, and he will make straight your paths" (Prov 3:5-6). Trusting in
the Lord is like placing our hand firmly in His. If we trust Him, He
will guide us.

While I was writing this book, I was contemplating a marriage
proposal and my heart was under a great deal of pressure to come to a
decision soon. I needed to practice what I was writing about: patience,
prayer, trust in the Lord, listening to one's heart, following the "compass" of one's joy and peace, constantly seeking to do what best stirs us
to love, etc. This process of discerning God's will is not something that
ends once one has chosen a path in life. It is a lifelong process. And it
is certainly not always easy.

I have learned that sometimes we have to wait a long time, with
patience and total confidence, for God's will to be made known to us.
We are given these perfect opportunities to practice perseverance in
hope and to walk by "the luminous torch of faith"[50] as the Lord is
working and preparing His ways.

Father Conrad wrote to me that "every vocation ... consists of an
element of *desire* (placed in our hearts by God's providence), an element of personal *decision*, and an element of *acceptance* by the other(s).
In the case of marriage, one must be 'accepted' by the one who is desired as a spouse; or in the case of the religious life, one must be 'accepted' by the religious community. And the realization of every vocation
has also its deal of suffering.... Be sure that Jesus is absolutely present,
even in the darkness [of not knowing what He wills for us]. From your

mind to your heart, where He is living, the distance is only twenty centimeters! Heaven is there!"

Father Conrad also counseled me that as I sought with all my heart to know God's will, I should tell Our Lord often of my love for Him. He will guide us faithfully all the way. "He is not sleeping in your heart, He is very awake! And very divine. And very eternal," Father told me. We might have to go through a time of purification before being graced with the knowledge of His will for our lives, but we will see, sooner or later, that His plans for us were worth waiting and suffering for.

Saint Paul told us so beautifully: "Have no anxiety about anything, but in everything by prayer and supplication with thanksgiving let your requests be made known to God. And the peace of God, which passes all understanding, will keep your hearts and your minds in Christ Jesus" (Phil 4:6,7).

We Are All Called to Be "Missionaries of Charity"

*They were poor in earthly things, but very rich
in grace and virtues.*
SAINT THOMAS À KEMPIS

Mother Teresa named her religious Order the "Missionaries of Charity" because, in essence, this name means "carriers of God's love." Since my first encounters with Mother Teresa and her Sisters, I have sensed that we are *all* called to this same purpose, whether we wear a religious habit and live in a convent, or whether we are "missionaries of charity in disguise," wearing ordinary clothes and living in ordinary homes, yet carrying that same love, joy, and goodness to others. Each of us, no matter what our state in life, has the mission and purpose of bringing God's love and peace to those around us.

The members of this religious Order are like a big family spread throughout the world. Mother Teresa said she would give saints to the Church from among her missionary Sisters and Brothers, and I firmly believe she has been doing this from the very beginning. The Missionaries of Charity are truly on a path to great sanctity.

The Sisters come from many different countries throughout the world and from all levels of society. They are doctors' daughters and children of peasants. Some are extremely well-educated. Many are young, especially at heart. All have a certain inner strength and cheerfulness about them. They possess a joy that is contagious. Each one has great faith, for they have given up their families, their friends, their jobs, their homes, and in many cases their countries in order to follow Christ.

There are important prerequisites to becoming Mother Teresa's followers. Sister Priscilla, who is presently one of the leading officials in the Community, explained a few: "First the girls must have a spirit of joy and cheerfulness in the work to be able to lift the people up out of their sufferings; then, they must have the spirit of work. Our constitution says that 'we must labor for the poor,' so it's not just ordinary hard work — it's real labor. We have many vocations in our Society and I think it's because the girls are looking for a challenge. They want a life of poverty, a life of sacrifice, they want to serve the poor, they want Jesus, they want a life of prayer."[51]

Actually, to become a Missionary of Charity, one must meet four specific conditions:

- Must be healthy of mind and body;
- Must have the ability to learn;
- Must have plenty of common sense; and
- Must have a cheerful disposition.

Mother Teresa would tell the Sisters: "Keep smiling. To be a real Missionary of Charity you must be a cheerful sufferer." They give their entire selves completely to God and to others through love, and the fruit of this total gift of self is joy — a very radiant and visible joy!

In the documentary film *Mother Teresa* by Ann and Jeanette Petrie, Mother said:

Very often people mistake the work with the vocation. The work is *not* the vocation. The vocation is to belong to Jesus. The aim of our Congregation, the reason for our existence, is to satiate the thirst of Jesus for love for souls. That was the last human cry of Jesus on the Cross: "I thirst." It was not so much the thirst for water, ordinary water; it was the thirst for your love, for my love, and for the love for one another.

Humanly speaking, what the Sisters are doing is out of the question; but once you realize Whom you are touching, Whom you are loving, that makes the difference. Jesus very clearly said: "I was hungry, you gave Me to eat; I was naked, you clothed Me; I was homeless, you took Me in; I was lonely, you consoled Me...." [This is] Dear Jesus in the distressing disguise of the poor.

This point is so important that I wish to share another explanation of it by Mother Teresa herself, for she did not want people to view her work simply as social work. It was much more than that:

All we do — our prayer, our work, our suffering — is for Jesus. Our life has no other reason or motivation. This is a point many people do not understand. I serve Jesus twenty-four hours a day. Whatever I do is for Him. And He gives me strength. I love Him in the poor and the poor in Him. But always the Lord comes first. Whenever a visitor comes to our house, I take him to the chapel to pray awhile. I tell him: "Let us first greet the Master of the house. Jesus is here." It is for Him we work, to Him we devote ourselves. He gives us the strength to carry on this life and to do so with happiness. Without Him, we could not do what we do. We certainly could not continue doing it for a whole lifetime. One year, two years, perhaps; but not during a whole life, without thought of reward, without expectation of anything good except to suffer with Him Who loved us so much that He gave His life for us. Without Jesus our life would be meaningless, incomprehensible. Jesus explains our life.[52]

"The work is very, very beautiful.... We have no reason to be unhappy. We are doing it with Jesus, for Jesus, to Jesus," Mother Teresa said. "In my work, I belong to the whole world. But in my heart, I belong to Christ."

It takes about nine-and-a-half years to become a full-fledged Missionary of Charity. Each woman has to go through stages of training and spiritual development. It is a long, arduous, but very beautiful journey. The stimulus, the inspiration, the courage, and the strength to go through all of this "comes from Christ and the Sacrament," Mother Teresa explained. "Without Him, we could do nothing." This makes sense because "God is Love" and "Love can do all things and the most difficult things don't appear difficult to it."[53]

In Calcutta, Mother Teresa used to send the new arrivals, the prospective Sisters, to the Home for the Dying on their very first day. This was a rule. She taught them to care for Jesus in the broken, bruised bodies of the dying with the same tenderness and love with which the priest touches Jesus in the Sacred Host at Mass. If they could not handle this, then they might as well go home, because this level of service is the very heart of their work. The Sisters must be able to see Our Lord in every human being, especially in His most distressing disguise of the Poorest of the Poor. Mother Teresa would tell the young novices straight away that if they didn't have the heart to serve the destitute and dying that they should go home. She did not need large numbers of Sisters, she would say; she needed hearts burning with love.

Several young novices and I carrying some of the children in the courtyard at the orphanage. Sisters wearing white saris *without* the blue trim are the young Sisters in training, the novices. Their days are organized into times to eat, work, pray, rest, and enjoy recreation. Sometimes you can hear their laughter all the way down the street from the convent!

The Sisters are able to remain in this challenging way of love because they know that God wants them to be there; if they did not believe this, they could hardly continue. God wills it and God sustains them. There is no other explanation. If this were merely social work rather than a deeply religious vocation, there would be a high turnover rate among them. They would get "burnt out" in their rigorous work and unrelenting schedule. They would lose heart. Instead, there seems to be the same intensity of love and joy in the Sisters who have been with the Order for forty and fifty years as there is in those who have just joined. It is a bit of a miracle, a mystery. "This is our life together with Jesus," Mother Teresa said. She taught the Sisters to cling to Christ, to cleave to Him, as young newlyweds cling to each other and become one. And this makes all the difference.

Mother Teresa said that in order to persevere in doing this work for a long time, "You need a greater power to push you from behind. Only religious life can give this power.... How necessary it is that we be religious for this work." She used to pray, especially during more difficult times: "My God give me courage now, this moment, to persevere in doing Your will." The Sisters lived lives of selfless devotion to God and to the poor, the sick, the unwanted and abandoned, the unnoticed and homeless, the destitute and dying, the "untouchables" of society. Like Mother Teresa herself, they did not need to use any words at all to teach us about faith and compassion. We only needed to look at their lives and we could see what their faith was all about.

My respect for the Missionaries of Charity was enormous because, although I shared in the work, I was able to go home after the summer months were over. These missionaries, on the other hand, had given their whole lives to this work. The rest of their earthly existence would be lived in these conditions. I could endure the floods, the stench, the bugs, the unbearable heat, the filth, and all the rest because I could see the light at the end of the tunnel. I could count the days when I would be walking through the kitchen door at home and be embraced by my family, when I could sleep again in my own comfortable, clean bed, when I could drink fresh, clean water again, when I could breathe fresh, clean air and smell the Maine pine trees, flowers, and ocean. These Sisters did not see the same light at the end of their tunnel. Their light was the Eternal One in heaven, not on earth. What I did and what I gave in Calcutta was nothing compared to what they are doing and giving. The Missionaries of Charity give their all to God and to our brothers and sisters in need. They do not hold anything back and they never stop. Their only reward in this life is the joy of living a holy life and serving Jesus in the Poorest of the Poor.

I have such a deep admiration for the way that these Missionaries of Charity live their lives and give their lives. They keep nothing for themselves. Geoffrey Moorhouse said, "They are exposed to every disease in the city, they work preposterous hours, they are not encouraged to spare themselves." They are sent all over the world, to the very poorest areas, to do God's work of love with great joy, humility, and grace. They are a tremendous inspiration to me. It is very humbling to think of them and all that they do, because in comparison, what I do is so small. We volunteers shared in their work for a time, and we sacrificed the comfort of home and family and conveniences, but eventually we returned to everything that makes life so pleasant and easy. These Sisters *never* go back to comfortable homes or easy lives. Their sacrifices are life-long, radical, and complete. Theirs makes ours look like no sacrifice at all. What they give to Jesus is nothing less than everything.

Mother Teresa used to speak about the "freedom of poverty," which, at first glance, seems like a contradiction of terms. She said: "The Sisters are always smiling and happy. We are so free, we are so free. I think people are so preoccupied with material difficulties. In the industrial world where people are supposed to have so much, I find that many people, while dressed up, are really, really poor. By having nothing, we will be able to give everything — through the freedom of poverty."[54]

Mother Teresa was not exaggerating in the least when she said that they take their vow of poverty very seriously. Their life is a challenge, a real labor of love. They scrub the floors on their hands and knees, for instance, and they do their laundry by hand in buckets of water. There are no modern conveniences, and they never take vacations. "To serve well our poor, we must understand them; to understand their poverty, we must experience it…. Our Sisters must feel as they feel, feel their poverty before God, know what it is to live without security, depending on God for the morrow." Mother Teresa insisted: "Our life of poverty is as necessary as the work itself." Their personal possessions include so little, and yet the Sisters will tell you, especially by their smiles,

"We have what we need." Sister Priscilla believes that a life of real poverty is what keeps the Order vibrant, young — and thriving. These young people are looking for a challenge and looking for real ways in which to express their love for God. Following in Mother Teresa's footsteps, they have found what they were looking for.

To her Sisters, Mother Teresa would say: "We must be proud of being poor.... If you have to sleep in a corner where there is no breeze, do not gasp and pant to show how much you feel it. In these little things one can practice poverty. Poverty makes us free. That is why we can joke and smile and keep a happy heart for Jesus.... Keep to the simple ways of poverty, of repairing your own shoes, and so forth, in short, of loving poverty as you love your mother. Our Society will live as long as that real poverty exists."[55]

"Being Together Is Our Strength"

Alone we can do nothing, but together we can do something beautiful for God.
MOTHER TERESA

"We all belong to the same family," Mother Teresa said. We are all God's children, and all people were welcome to join her in her work for the Poorest of the Poor. "Christians, Muslims, Hindus, believers and nonbelievers have the opportunity with us to do works of love, have the opportunity with us to share the joy of loving and coming to realize God's presence. Hindus become better Hindus. Catholics become better Catholics. Muslims become better Muslims."

Some volunteers, like myself, came with no special expertise except what Mother Teresa called "a joyful willingness to do the most humble work for the sick and dying." Like the Sisters, we came from all different backgrounds and from all areas of the earth. My Calcutta friends and acquaintances included a medical student from Sweden, a teacher from Australia, a truck driver from England, a businessman from France, and young college students from America. We each stayed as long as we could, or as long as our savings lasted! We became like brothers and sisters to one another. We would gather at mealtimes and in the evenings to share stories about our personal lives and tales about our daily experiences in Calcutta. "The chatter around the breakfast table was just a babble of foreign languages," one volunteer from Australia wrote, "but everyone was happy." It was like the family of mankind gathered in this one special place. The friendships that formed between us have been enduring ones, continuing long after the Calcutta experience ended and we each returned to our own countries.

There were several young people volunteering in Calcutta who, in their own countries, were studying to become medical experts. They did not learn a great deal about medicine in the Home for the Dying, but they learned a lot about the compassion side of being a doctor or nurse.

Meeting volunteers from all over the world was a priceless part of this experience. Mother Teresa's open invitation to serve the poor brought the world together. We really grew to love one another as we worked side-by-side, trying to comfort the afflicted, giving all we had to give, and bringing out the best in one another. "Experience teaches us that love does not consist of two people looking at each other, but of looking together in the same direction," said Antoine de Saint-Exupéry.

Close to Mother Teresa, a living saint, and close to the poor, who were saints in their own right, each volunteer was able to witness the

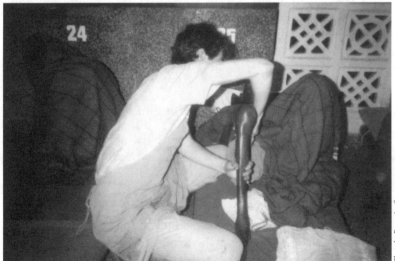

Photo by Bruce Aguilar

A young American volunteer, Scott Abernathy, helps exercise the legs of one of the male patients in the Home for the Dying.

inspiring greatness of human potential. We were becoming, in Mother Teresa's words, "a better Hindu, a better Muslim, a better Catholic, a better whatever we were, and then by being better we were coming closer and closer to God."

I wrote to my family from Calcutta: "Time continues to fly. Although I will return home with open arms and a big smile, I find myself clinging to the remaining days here, wishing that they would not pass by so quickly. I still have so much more to learn and to do before leaving. In this place, where volunteers can receive Holy Communion at daily Mass, serve God 'in His distressing disguise of the poor,' and adore Him every evening in the Blessed Sacrament, I find that we are being fed spiritually like never before. Every moment offers opportunities for prayer, sacrifice, reflection, service, and sharing — whether I am kneeling in the chapel praying, or sitting quietly at the bedside of a dying patient just holding his hand. Every breath is a prayer. Every difficult sight, sound, or task becomes a beautiful offering of love."

Mother Teresa said it most beautifully: "Sharing and thoughtfulness help build community life. Doing small things for the great love of each other: maybe just a smile, maybe just carrying a bucket of water, maybe just thoughtfulness at the table. These are small things, small things. And that continual sharing with each other, continual relating to each other — Mass together, Eucharist together, adoration together, doing penance together — to be able to share the suffering and understand the suffering of our people. We really do everything together, and I think that being together is our strength."[56]

We All Have Something to Share

Use the beautiful gifts God has given you for His greater glory. All that you have and all that you are and all that you can be and do....
MOTHER TERESA

The personalities and gifts of the individuals who were brought together in Calcutta were infinitely rich in diversity. Each person was so unique, and this is what made the "bouquet" of volunteers and Sisters so appealing. One person's talents did not diminish the value of another's talents. Our gifts enhanced and complemented one another, or as Saint Thérèse said: "The splendor of the rose and the whiteness of the lily do not rob the little violet of its scent, nor the daisy of its simple charm."

Moira was a volunteer from Australia who was best at working with young children and making everyone laugh. Ordinarily she worked at the orphanage; I did not see her enter the shelter for dying destitutes until the Fourth of July. When she came in, she brought with her a guitar! I'd never seen anyone with a guitar in Home for the Dying. Moira went into the women's section where I was caring for one of the patients. She sat down on one of the empty beds and began to play her guitar and sing. In her usual fashion, her joy and enthusiasm bubbled over onto everyone in the room. I will never forget the sight of Nirmal Hriday that afternoon. There were smiles, tapping toes, and new life. "If you're happy and you know it, clap your hands," she sang, and dozens of patients along with the volunteers were joining in. Then she started singing the "Hokey Pokey," and one of the patients who looked like a living skeleton actually got up out of her bed and began to do the

My fun-loving volunteer friend Paul from Ireland pulls me, our rickshaw driver (center), and our friend Brigit from Holland around the driveway at the small guesthouse near the Motherhouse and the orphanage. Paul and Brigit married in February 2001.

Hokey Pokey in the middle of the aisle with one of the volunteers! She put her left foot in, and took her left foot out — I could hardly believe my eyes. Those who had the strength to clap their hands were doing so, and those who could not clap were at least smiling and laughing. With her music, Moira brought great life and spirit into this home. I found myself wishing that I had the gift of music to share, because I could see how much happiness it brought to others.

While Moira was entertaining us, I glanced over at another volunteer, Teresa, from Canada. Independent, strong-spirited, practical, and sensible; I had so much respect for her. She was so efficient at cleaning up messes, changing the diaper-cloths of the patients, and distributing medicines. She had guts, courage, and fierce determination. During Moira's performance, a destitute woman had soiled her garments and I watched Teresa, as if in a military drill, get a pail of warm water and clean, dry garments; she rolled up her sleeves and proceeded to do this dirty work with such ease and skill that I found myself wishing that I had that same gift. Yes, I cleaned up messes too; I did the exact work that she was doing, but I could not do it nearly as well as she did. I was more delicate and not as efficient or courageous. I was silently choked by the awful stench, whereas Teresa did not seemed phased by it. She got right down to business, without flinching!

So there I sat at my patient's side, rubbing her arms, trying to alleviate at least part of her suffering, and from time to time looking over at Moira with her guitar wishing that I could bring happiness in the way that she was; then looking over at Teresa, wishing that I could work as efficiently and unstintingly as she could when, all of a sudden, a patient in the bed next to me started crying out in agony. Moira heard the crying, put down her guitar, and came over to assist this poor woman. She sat next to her, took her hand and tried to comfort her but, within just a couple of minutes, Moira became very uneasy with the situation and had to get up and leave. She did not know how to do it. She was not accustomed to seeing such intense human suffering. She seemed afraid to look closely at someone who was dying. And I realized: *ah- ha*! This is *my* gift! I can sit at a patient's bedside and look into her eyes and stay with her in her agony no matter how intense, and truly be with her in her suffering.

Here I'm with some of my beloved volunteer friends — (left to right) Paul from Sweden, Valerie from Canada and Adam (Paul's brother) with Mother Teresa at the Motherhouse. She had given all of us Miraculous Medals, and we were each wearing them close to our hearts, as she wanted us to do.

I learned a valuable lesson that day. I learned that we all have something to share. Even if my gift is simply "hands to serve and a heart to love," it is still a good and useful gift, and it is important to use it for the good of others. I peacefully realized that it is all right if we all cannot play the guitar like Moira can; it is okay if we all cannot clean up the messes as efficiently as Teresa can. Each person has gifts, and the important thing is that each of us is giving what we have to give, sharing whatever God has blessed us with. "The world of our souls is like a garden in the eyes of God," Saint Thérèse taught, and there is infinite *variety* of goodness and talent in each of us, just as there is an infinite variety of colors, fragrances, textures, sizes, and shapes of flowers. Holiness does not mean we each have to be a rose; "if every flower were a rose, springtime would lose its loveliness!" Instead, "holiness consists in being what we are meant to be," and sharing what we are meant to share.

Mother said: "It is so beautiful that we complete each other! What we are doing in the slums, maybe you cannot do. What you are doing at the level where you are called — in your family life, in your college life, in your work — we cannot do. But you and we together are doing something beautiful for God."

"Now there are varieties of gifts, but the same Spirit," Saint Paul wrote; "there are varieties of service, but the same Lord; there are different works, but there are varieties of working, and it is the same God who inspires them all in every one. To each is given the manifestation of the Spirit for the common good.... All these are inspired by one and the same Spirit, who apportions to each one individually as he wills" (1Cor 12:4-7,11). How important it is for us to pay close heed to what Saint Paul said next as he beckoned us to "earnestly desire the higher gifts" (1Cor 12:31). He wrote so beautifully about the excellence of the gift of LOVE:

> And I will show you a still more excellent way. If I speak in the tongues of men and of angels, but have not love, I am a noisy gong or a clanging cymbal. And if I have prophetic powers, and understand all mysteries and all knowledge, and if I have all faith, so as to remove mountains, but have not love, I am nothing. If I give away all I have, and if I deliver my body to be burned, but have not love, I gain nothing.
>
> Love is patient and kind; love is not jealous or boastful; it is not arrogant or rude. Love does not insist on its own way; it is not irritable or resentful; it does not rejoice at wrong, but rejoices in the right. Love bears all things, believes all things, hopes all things, endures all things. Love never ends (1 Cor 12:31;13:1-8).

Mother Teresa demonstrated that this is what life is all about. My next challenge was to bring these lessons of love home with me.

Chapter Eight

✿

Bringing Home Mother Teresa's Lessons

The world's "most admired woman" had a profound impact on *millions* of lives — princes and paupers, presidents and popes, the Poorest of the Poor and countless ordinary people like me. Her appeal was universal. Her love was for everybody. She was like a mother to multitudes of people throughout the world. Everything she did was filled with total love and commitment, unfaltering faith, warmth, and sincerity. Moments in her presence were unforgettable. This is why, when it came time to part from her at the end of the summer, my smiles turned into tears.

Farewell to Calcutta

The most difficult part of my experience in Calcutta was leaving, saying farewell to the children, the dying patients, the Sisters, the other volunteers from around the world, and of course, Mother Teresa herself. With them, I felt as though I had lived a lifetime of fulfillment.

I could hardly believe that my dream of being in Calcutta, India, working for Mother Teresa and the Poorest of the Poor had actually come true. My experience far surpassed my dreams in beauty, enrichment, and fulfillment. Before coming to Calcutta, I wanted only to hold one dying destitute's hand and comfort even just *one* soul; I wanted to leave some small, lasting contribution such as a single painting to hang on the wall; I hoped and prayed simply to have the chance just to *see* Mother Teresa, simply to lay eyes on her. As it turned out, I was blessed over and over again with opportunities to speak with her, hold her hand, receive God's blessings from her, do personal favors for her, and even tell her that I loved her. I never imagined that this experience would be so wonderful and fulfilling.

While parting with Mother Teresa, I felt much like Malcolm Muggeridge did in similar circumstances. He said he felt as if he was leaving behind "all the beauty and all the joy in the universe" when Mother Teresa rode away. "God's universal love has rubbed off on Mother Teresa, giving her homely features a noticeable luminosity, a shining quality. She has lived so closely with Our Lord that the same enchantment clings about her that sent the crowds chasing after Him...."

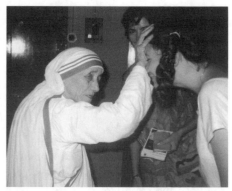

Here, Mother Teresa gives a farewell blessing to my friend Jane Clement. Mother gave each of us her special blessing for a safe journey home to America. This was when she gave me one of the little prayer books used by the Missionaries of Charity, and inside the cover she wrote: "Be only all for Jesus through Mary."

When I left Mother Teresa in Calcutta after the summer was over, it was a bittersweet experience. I was sad to leave, yet incredibly excited to be going home. I began my long journey back to the United States with a heart full of mixed emotions.

A Warm Welcome Home

I knelt down and kissed the grass when I arrived home, saying, "God Bless America — land that I love!"
MY DIARY, AUGUST 29, 1986

A recurrent theme in my dear mother's letters to me while I was away in India was that her happiest day would be when I came through her kitchen doors again and was safely in her arms. Her happiest day was coming *soon*!

When I flew into Boston, after five flights across the world from India, I received a warm welcome from my brother Brian, his wife Linda, and my sister Ruthie, who had come to Logan Airport to pick me up. I made a long-distance call to my parents in Maine from the airport. I think Dad was crying when I told him that I was on my way home from Boston.

Mama had packed my favorite homemade muffins for me, with a special note to welcome me home. She always adds the most thoughtful touches! I devoured a couple of muffins immediately. My siblings began asking questions about my trip, and I happily began telling my stories.

Finally, I arrived home-sweet-home after so long, and after so much had happened. There I found more warm, long embraces. My youngest sister Margie and Mama and Papa were there waiting for me with open arms. There was a lavender vase filled with a lovely arrangement of fresh flowers and a red rose from Paul (my Swedish friend) with an accompanying letter that I saved for a day or two until things settled down a bit and I could sit alone and read it in peace. The flowers really melted my heart and brought a big smile to my face.

My mother went with me upstairs to my room, where I found three big bright balloons on which were written "Welcome Home, Sweet Sue!" I also found a new, hard-covered book on Mother Teresa with a special heart-warming inscription inside the cover from Mom and Dad. On the nightstand was a note that read: "We love you, Sue Sue...." It was a blessing to be home!

It Seemed Like Calcutta Had Only Been a Dream

The next morning I woke up in my own bed at home in Maine, and my entire experience in Calcutta seemed like just a dream....

I wrote in my diary: "I am back with my loved ones now, safe and sound, clean, secure, well-fed, loved, housed, protected, and worry-free. I am breathing fresh, clean air again, drinking cool, clear water, savoring the natural beauty and splendor of Maine, which has surrounded me all my life. It is so strange ... after living in a poverty-stricken, struggling city like Calcutta, India."

Day after day, I continued to rejoice in the great feeling of being home after such a beautiful experience. I would wake up early, as the sun was rising so beautifully, and notice the trees changing color, some of the leaves turning deep, rich, gorgeous fall tones. I so enjoyed following and appreciating the changing of seasons, with the special beauty that each one brings. In Calcutta, the only natural beauty to be found (aside from the beauty in the people themselves) was in the billowing, majestic clouds overhead, and in the wide-open blue sky. There is so much to appreciate here in the United States, so much heavenly splendor in the great outdoors.

Unless I took the time to recall all that I experienced in Calcutta that summer, unless I made the effort to bring it all back to mind, I feared my memories of Calcutta would be lost. It would be so easy to slip back into my own culture and lose the memories of this distant one. The thought of losing these memories concerned me. These experiences were much too precious, too special, too important in my life, too enriching and meaningful to be lost. That is why my photographs are so treasured; they will not let me forget. It is far too easy to live in this Western world, which in no way, shape, or manner resembles the world in which I lived during that summer, without thinking twice about the hellish struggle of life in cities like Calcutta. I never want to forget what I lived and learned, those whom I loved and cared for, all that I saw, felt, said and did, or even what I touched, tasted, smelled, and stepped in! I never want to lose sight of the beauty, peace, love, and joy I found amidst the ugliness, struggle, suffering, poverty, and death in Calcutta.

I felt a need to remind myself why it was such a beautiful, fulfilling, and joy-filled experience when I was living amidst such miserable conditions and such hell. What made this "Black Hole" so thoroughly pleasing and even pacifying is important to keep always in mind, for these are the basic ingredients of a happy, fulfilling life. My summer-long experience in Calcutta has strongly reinforced my belief that loving others is what life is all about. Reaching out, helping, and serving others is our life's purpose. Loving others, especially those who are in most need, brings me such joy. When I tried to *give* love and joy, I ended up *receiving* far more from the dying destitutes, from the precious children, from my friends, from Mother Teresa, and from the lovely Sisters. If my life resembles in any way my summer-long experiences with the Missionaries of Charity, with these carriers of God's love, and if I try to live as I did this summer, intent on giving, sharing, loving, emptying myself out for others, with the same results, then I will, as I have always dreamed, live *happily ever after...* for it is in giving that we receive, it is in forgetting self that we find, and it is in sharing joy and peace that we feel the greatest depth of joy and peace and the love of God in our own hearts.

I brought home three packages of "Milk Bikis" biscuits from New Delhi, India, to share with my family and let them taste the kind of cookies I had eaten all summer in India. Well, I opened up a package and spotted a little baby COCKROACH on top of the first cookie! I thought it was hysterically funny, because it was so typical of what I had experienced in Calcutta. Dad, however, was not as tickled as I was by a cockroach on a cookie. He was absolutely disgusted, and he made me throw them all away.

My oldest sister Kathie wouldn't allow me to hold her newborn baby Cindy because she was afraid that I might transmit some strange disease or germs from India. She feared I carried diseases to which I might have built up strong immunity and resistance, but to which little Cindy would fall prey. I fully understood how Kathie felt and exactly why she was concerned. She was 100 percent justified in her request that I not get too close to her little angel until I had a thorough physical examination. Nevertheless, I felt sort of like a leper, feared and possibly carrying a contagious and dreadful illness. I felt as if I had been quarantined, as if I was dangerous. It was a strange feeling, one that I had never felt before. I understood, but in a funny sort of way, it still hurt a bit to be treated and thought of in that way.

I kept pondering all that I had seen and learned in Calcutta, and wrote about it in my journal:

My diary, September 7: *The Poorest of the Poor don't really ask for much and they are often satisfied with so little. We have so much to learn from people like these. Having lived amongst them, I question more earnestly our own pursuits and aspirations; I examine them more critically. What disturbs me greatly about my own world is the all-encompassing image-consciousness: What kind of car do you drive? What kind of work do you do? What salary do you make? Do you live in a big house? Do you travel? Play tennis? Belong to a club? Own fifty pairs of shoes? Dress stylishly? Who cares? I'm not impressed by the things that are considered by many to be impressive. Another thing that disturbs me personally is the wastefulness of our Western world. Just minutes ago, I watched on television fresh dairy farm milk draining from tanks onto the ground. I watched in utter disbelief as a farmer spoke about the dropping milk prices and the futility of negotiation. . . . I glared at the stream of milk flowing down a hillside and wondered at the ignorance, waste, and selfishness in this day and age, in a world where poverty and starvation still exist amidst the wealth, surplus, and well-being. I don't understand. It angers and grieves me to the core of my being. I want to scream out in protest of this hideous wastefulness and this selfishness. . . .*

I guess I see the waste and selfishness so much more clearly now because I have traveled from a land of poverty back to a land of plenty. We do have so much.

Returning to Dartmouth

One minute I was giving an injection to a dying woman from the slums of Calcutta, and the next thing I knew I was back on campus, studying Economics at Dartmouth.
MY DIARY, SEPTEMBER 12

It truly was a joy to be back home in the United States, to breathe fresh, clean air again, to walk barefoot through plush, green grass, and to stroll along the old, familiar sandy beaches of Maine. It was wonderful, finally, to be able to escape all the noise and confusion, and to find peaceful silence. It was great to be back in my parents' arms again, to relieve them of all their anxiety and fear. I must add, however, that upon arrival at New York's JFK Airport, and on my way to Boston, I sensed an inner emptiness and, for a moment, a real longing to return to Calcutta, where I had lived such an uncomplicated, deeply meaningful existence working with the Poorest of the Poor.

Suddenly it had ended, my Calcutta experience and lifestyle. It was as if the clock had struck twelve and I was all at once back in my own world, as if I had never even been away. A major portion of my life had just crystallized in an extraordinarily beautiful pattern. I had lived a long-held dream.

Upon my return from India, my goal was to finish my studies and graduate from Dartmouth. My Calcutta experience took place during the summer between my junior and senior years at college, so when I returned home, I had some "unfinished business": one more year of school. And this was a great blessing. I see now that, without the structure and direction of school in my life, it would have been easy to become "lost" and confused in our culture after experiencing something so intense and so radically different. Even though my heart was no longer interested in learning Economics, it really was too late to change my major. Besides, I really felt that it was important to finish what I had begun. Actually, I had very little time to ponder my future or to become confused — I literally had only days at home before I had to return to college in Hanover, New Hampshire.

This was a drastic change for me: one day I was in the Home for Dying Destitutes in Calcutta feeding emaciated patients, and the next thing I knew I was back on campus, in that "perfect little world" of Dartmouth, surrounded by healthy, strong, intelligent, happy young people, enjoying the greenest grass in the world, brilliant sunshine, gorgeous mountains in the distance, fresh air, lovely buildings, so much hope, abundant peacefulness, a world of opportunity for all…. THIS was the culture shock! — not *going* to India, but rather *coming back home* from India. We have everything we could ever want, all at our fingertips. The amazing thing is that we do not even *realize* how blessed we are. I felt like standing on the rooftops and shouting to everyone on campus, to everyone in this country:

> We are so fortunate! Please let's *count* our blessings and *thank God* for them, because these blessings are so great and wonderful. Not everybody in the world has the things that we so easily take for granted. We have everything, and millions of people have absolutely nothing. Please *realize* this and at least be *grateful* for what you have.

I wanted everyone to be full of contentment and awareness of how abundantly blessed each of us is. Gratitude is one of the greatest secrets of happiness. A grateful heart has no room for complaining, whining, restlessness, or sadness. It is too busy being thankful and happy.

In my first letter to Mother Teresa after my return to the United States, I tried to acknowledge all that I had received from her, and I also extended a personal invitation to her:

Dearest Mother Teresa,

Please accept my heartfelt thanks and love and appreciation for all that you have done — not only for me but for the many others whose lives you have touched so deeply…. It meant so much to me to hear you say those three simple words: "God bless you." What more could anyone ask for? What more do we need than God's blessings? …I have something special to ask you, Mother Teresa. I would like to invite you to come to Dartmouth College here in the United States this spring. The students here would so enjoy hearing you speak of love, poverty, service to others, peace and joy … and life in the Spirit.

We will soon be graduating from college and entering into the working world. It is so important for us to be reminded of the beauty of reaching out and working for others, rather than working solely for money or for ourselves. It was a very special privilege to hear you speak of such things when I was in Calcutta, and because it meant so much to me, I would love to share you and your inspiring words with all of the young college students here at Dartmouth…. I see how brightly and warmly Our Lord shines through you. I want others to see and know that each one of us can be a lantern burning with God's love. I want others to know also that holiness is within reach of us all — that it is not limited to just a few. Every one of us needs to be reminded of this.

Father Bill is the priest here at Saint Thomas Aquinas Church, where I attend Mass. He told me that we could meet you at the airport and provide accommodations for you during your stay, if you could come. We would take very special care of you, Mother, even though I know that Jesus takes very tender, loving care of you Himself! If you could somehow speak to us this spring, we would feel well-blessed and honored, to say the least. Whether or not you are able to visit and speak to us, I want you to know how deeply touched I am by the encounters I had in Calcutta with the Poor. I will always be touched by your example of Christ's love. You light up my life, Mother, and I love you dearly. My thoughts and prayers are with you and the Missionaries of Charity. May you continue to carry God's love and peace to the Poorest of the Poor, knowing in your heart the richness and tenderness of Christ's love for you.

May God bless you, Mother Teresa, and keep you in his tender, loving care.

Sincerely in Christ Jesus,
Susan

Mother Teresa responded to my invitation to come and speak at Dartmouth, and she assured us of her prayers: "Due to many more pressing needs and prior commitments, I am sorry I will not be able to accept your invitation to Dartmouth College in April or May. I will pray in a special way for you and the others that after graduation you may reach out to the poor in the world — by being the sunshine of His love. My prayer for you is that you may grow more and more in His likeness through love and compassion and so become an instrument of peace... (Mother Teresa's letter, dated March 10, 1987).

"Stay Where You Are, Find Your Own Calcutta"

You can find Calcutta all over the world, if you have eyes to see. Everywhere, wherever you go, you find people who are unwanted, unloved, uncared for, just rejected by the society — completely forgotten, completely left alone. That is the greatest poverty of the rich countries.

MOTHER TERESA, IN THE DOCUMENTARY FILM,

MOTHER TERESA

When Mother Teresa was in the United States she spoke at Harvard University, saying: "You will, I'm sure, ask me: 'Where is that hunger in our country? Where is that nakedness in our country? Where is that homelessness in our country?' Yes, there *is* hunger. Maybe not hunger for a piece of bread, but there is a terrible hunger for *love*. We all experience that in our lives — the pain, the loneliness. We must have the courage to recognize the poor you may have right in your own family. Find them, love them, put your love for them into living action — for in loving them, you are loving God Himself." Calcutta is everywhere. The need for love is all around us. "Most of the time people don't even know of the existence of the poor," Mother Teresa said. "We look and we don't see."[57]

We do not need to go to far-off lands to find basic human needs or to be a light to others. We are called to be a light right here, where we are. Mother Teresa used to tell us not to search for God in distant places — "He is not there," she would say. "He is close to you. He is with you. Just keep the lamp [of love in your heart] burning and you will always see Him. Watch and pray. Keep kindling the lamp and you will

"Stay where you are, find your own Calcutta."
Mother Teresa

Photo by Rik Daze

see His love and you will see how sweet is the Lord you love."

After my experience in Calcutta, I spent some time in New York serving as a volunteer with the Missionaries of Charity in the South Bronx and Harlem. It was a little rougher in New York. A little tougher. And the poverty was different, but my experiences there were equally as intense and meaningful as my experiences in Calcutta. In New York, I came into contact with people with AIDS for the first time in my life. And I felt the presence of God as never before in my life. Mother Teresa pointed out that as soon as we open our hearts to love others and to love God, we will find Him. Felt or unfelt, He is always with us, just as the sun is always there in the sky shining, even when the clouds are blocking its rays. If our faith is cloudless, we will always experience "the sunshine of God's love," and if we are reaching out to others, we will be a channel of this inexhaustible love, like a big opening in the clouds, letting the light shine through.

Mother Teresa reminded us that the poverty in the more affluent countries is a much deeper poverty than what one witnesses in countries like India. In Calcutta, we could give a piece of bread to a man who was hungry and satisfy his hunger. He would be so content! In New York, it was different. It took more than bread to feed the poor. Their hunger was deeper. It was loneliness, emptiness, a feeling of being nothing to society. Mother Teresa explained that "these people are not hungry in the physical sense but they are starving in another way. They know they need something more than money, yet they don't know what it is. What they are missing really is a living relationship with God." In the West, the only way to satisfy the hunger is to make many visits to the lonely and outcast, to continue showing love and care. A piece of bread did not satisfy their need as it did in Calcutta, where there was more joy and peace in the people's hearts. I felt that the constant, lively human interaction among Calcutta's poor on the streets gave them a sense of belonging; many poor people slept beside each other on the pavement at night and talked with one another throughout the day. There was a togetherness. People in our cities, in contrast, seem so isolated from one another. Our poor seem to have no one to talk to. Even those who are not poor seem to lack that sense of belonging, that sense of community and of family. People are hidden away in their homes, in their own private rooms, or in their cardboard boxes. They seem more alone and lonely.

Once in a while, someone would write to Mother Teresa and ask for permission to come to Calcutta to help serve the Poorest of the Poor, and Mother Teresa would write back and say, "Stay where you are — find your own Calcutta. Find the sick, the suffering, the lonely right there where you are — in your own homes and in your own families, in your workplaces and schools." So often she told us to "start at home, at the level where you are called."

In a letter to her co-workers Mother said: "Look into your own homes, down your own streets." She wanted us to see the lonely, the suffering, the rejected, the drug addict, the depressed, the frightened, the sick, "and bring the love of God to people" as the Missionaries of Charity would do if they were there. "To all who suffer and are lonely, give always a happy smile. Give them not only your care but also your heart. Because of God's goodness and love, every moment of our life can be the beginning of great things." Mother Teresa's whole life attested to the truth of her words.

She always brought our attention back to our own families, and to those who are closest to us. In one of her letters to me, Mother Teresa wrote: "Remember, love begins at home. Jesus is waiting for your love and concern right where you are. Do you find Him in the hearts of your friends, neighbors — in your family? Look for the lonely, the unwanted, the unloved. Be God's light of love to them…. Keep sharing the joy of loving Jesus with everyone you meet through your kind words and your smile." She encouraged us to look around. "And find out about your next-door neighbors. Do you know who they are?"

"It is easy to love people far away," Mother Teresa said. "It is not always easy to love those close to us. It is easier to give a cup of rice to relieve hunger than to relieve the loneliness and pain of someone unloved in our own home. Bring love into your home, for this is where our love for each other must start."[58]

Home has always been the greatest classroom of love. It has always been the place where love is best taught, learned, and lived. "Start by making our own homes places where peace, happiness and love abound, through your love for each member of your family and for your neighbors," Mother Teresa would say. "Family first … because if you are not there … how will your love grow for one another?" Maybe our chil-

This picture of my youngest sister, Marjorie, with her husband, Matthew Boles, and two of their children, Sarah and Jacob, reminds me of something Mother Teresa said: "Meet each other with a smile. When it is difficult to smile, smile at each other. Make time for each other in your family."

dren, our husband, our wife, our brother or sister feels unwanted or unloved. "Let us look straight into our own families." On many occasions, Mother Teresa said: "I pray to bring back the tender love in a family. The family that prays together, stays together. If we stay together, we will love one another, as God loves each one of us."[59]

Mother Teresa inspired people to first take care of their *own* loved ones and try to make them happy. "First, do that, and then you may think of the poor of India and of other areas."

Bring God to Your Children

It is very important for children to hear their parents talk about God.
MOTHER TERESA

"The children must be able to ask about God…. If the parent sets the example, the children will not forget how to pray, how they love each other, how they share sorrow, how they share joy. Children watch … they watch and they grow with that. They will learn that it makes a difference how they live their lives by watching what the parents do."[60]

Mother Teresa emphasized that teaching children to pray and praying with them is a beautiful sign of love, a source of strength, peace, and unity in a family. "Prayer is needed for children. Whatever religion we are, we must pray together. Children need to learn to pray, and they need to have their parents pray with them. If we don't do this, it will be difficult to become holy, to carry on, to strengthen ourselves in faith."[61]

Parents and grandparents have the greatest opportunities to teach lasting lessons about love. The examples they give are the most powerful influence on young lives and hearts. When I was a child growing up as one of ten children, my mother used to show her love for us in countless ways. She was happy, gentle and full of peace — even amid the incessant activity and unrelenting demands of raising a large family. She stayed so loving and calm each day, and she was the heart of our home. The words of wisdom that she spoke remain as a light in my life, guiding my steps even to this day. She would often bake homemade cookies for our lunchboxes, and sometimes in the mornings she would bring warm cookies from the oven to us as we were upstairs getting ready for school. While I was at school, I could open up my sandwich any day and, seeing how well it was made, I could exclaim in my heart: "My Mama loves me!" This was so obvious in everything she did. She was never careless in the things she did for us. Everything, even the most mundane and simple things, like making our sandwiches, was done to perfection, and with tender love and care.

My father, likewise, gave us many lessons on charity and compassion. In quiet ways, he did "small things with great love." For example, every Sunday while I was growing up he assisted a gentleman from our parish who had Muscular Dystrophy. My father discovered why this man had not been coming inside for the celebration of the Mass — he was unable to get out of his car. As soon as my father discovered this, he offered to do something to help. Faithfully, each week, my dad would carry this gentleman in his arms from his car into the church; after placing him in the pew, my father would brace this man's legs so that he could stand during the Mass. After Mass was over, my father would again take him up into his arms and carry him from the church to his car. We did not think twice about this Sunday routine. It was not something that was ever discussed; it was just something that my father did. We also included this man in our family prayers each night. Not until I was much older did the beauty of my father's care register with me. I remembered my father with this grown man in his arms, carrying him in to worship God. I realized that my parents had been putting their love into living action all my life, within our family and outside our home. They did not need to use words to teach us about love. They were constantly giving us living *examples* of love.

Mother Teresa shared touching words about her mother's love for her husband:

> I'll never forget my own mother. She used to be very busy the whole day, but as soon as the evening came, she used to move very fast to get ready to meet my father. At that time we didn't understand; we used to smile; we used to laugh; and we used to tease her; but now I remember what a tremendous, delicate love she had for him. Didn't matter what happened, but she was ready there with a smile to meet him. Today we

have no time. The father and mother are so busy. The children come home and there's no one to love them, to smile at them.[62]

I keep discovering with Mother Teresa's missionaries that the meaning of life, the purpose of life … all boils down to LOVE. Mother Teresa used to remind us that at the end of our lives, we will not be judged on how much money we made, what kind of car we drove, or how many degrees we earned … we will be judged on how well we loved; how well we put our love into living action. Saint John of the Cross used to say, "The smallest act of pure love is of more value … than all other works together." His close friend, Saint Teresa of Ávila, wisely counseled, "Beg Our Lord to grant you perfect love…. He will give you more than you know how to desire."

One of the greatest challenges and responsibilities that I faced upon returning to the United States was keeping my Calcutta experience alive. I earnestly desired to continue practicing all that I had learned from Mother Teresa and to continue experiencing the same fullness of life and depth of joy. It was refreshing to me to hear Mother Teresa remind us that we did not need to tackle big things in order to experience this joy and to make a world of difference for those around us. She taught us to tend to the needs of one human being at a time. Her words and example were so encouraging: "I never look at the masses as my responsibility. I look at the individual. I can love only one person at a time. I can feed only one person at a time. Just one, one, one.…

"The whole work is only a drop in the ocean. But if I didn't put the drop in, the ocean would be one drop less. And that drop would be missed. Same thing for you, same thing for your family, same thing in the church where you go, just begin … one at a time."

"We must all fill our hearts with great love," Mother Teresa said. "Do not imagine that love to be true must be extraordinary. No, what we need in our love is the continuity to love the one we love. See how a lamp burns, by the continual consumption of the little drops of oil. If there are no more of these drops in the lamp, there will be no light.… What are these drops of oil in our lamps? They are the little things of everyday life: fidelity, punctuality, little words of kindness, just a little thought for others; those little acts of silence, of look, and of thought, of word, and of deed. These are the very drops of love that make our life burn with so much light."[63]

"The Greatest Disease in the World Today ... Is Being Unloved"

"I have come more and more to realize that ... it is being unwanted that is the worst disease that any human being can ever experience," Mother Teresa said. "For all kinds of diseases there are medicines and cures. But for being unwanted ... I don't think this terrible disease can ever be cured."

While writing this manuscript, a dear friend of mine, Father John Scahill, was dying in a local nursing home. He was an eighty-year-old retired priest who had served others until the very end of his life, until he literally could not stand anymore. Father Scahill loved people, and it was tremendously painful for him to be isolated in a nursing home during his last days. Each time I went to visit him, I was deeply moved by the sight of all the elderly men and women sitting in their wheelchairs waiting for love. "Please take me home!" one woman would cry out to me as I was leaving the nursing home.

There was another woman in a wheelchair who would look up at me and show an enormous smile whenever I simply said "Hi" to her. I would tell her what a beautiful smile she had and ask her to keep smiling until I came back for the next visit. People have told me that they hesitate to visit nursing homes or hospitals because they do not know what to say. We do not have to engage others in fancy conversation. We can always start with a smile or simply with the question, "How is your day?" It does not take much to bring a little sunshine into someone's day. Many people who are homebound or hospital-bound are dying just to have someone to speak to, someone to visit, someone to care about them. Just being there makes a difference. People everywhere are hungry for love, thirsting for someone to care. Mother Teresa always challenged us to have eyes that see and the courage and love to do something for those who are neglected in our society — the children, the elderly, the sick, the mentally ill, and the poor. There are people in our own families who feel unloved, depressed, and lonely.

Mother Teresa spoke of visiting a nursing home here in the West where so many of the elderly seemed to be forgotten. Mother saw in that home that "they had everything, beautiful things, but everybody was looking toward the door. And I did not see a single one with a smile on their face." She turned to one of her Sisters and asked how this could be. How could it be that these people who have everything are all looking toward the door? "Why are they not smiling?" Mother was used to seeing smiles on people; "even the dying ones smile." The Sister responded that the situation was like this nearly every day. "They are expecting, they are hoping that a son or daughter will come to visit them. They are hurt because they are forgotten." Mother Teresa's response was "And see — this is where *love* comes. That poverty comes right there in our own home, even a neglect to love. Maybe in our own family we have somebody who is feeling lonely, who is feeling sick, who is feeling worried, and these are difficult days for everybody. Are we there? Are we there to receive them?"

Mother Teresa always said that the poverty of being unwanted, unloved, uncared for, forgotten by everybody is a much greater poverty than the person who has nothing to eat. This type of hunger and poverty is very prevalent in our country.

One day, I walked into a local hospital and asked the director of volunteers if there were any patients there who were dying and had no one to visit them. I was given the name of an eighty-six-year-old woman named Mary Alice, and I was told that she was given about two weeks more to live. Mary Alice had been an only child; she had never married and she never had any children. She seemed entirely alone in the world, and here she was dying in a hospital with no one. I began to visit her daily, then twice a week. She called me her "Susie Q." Even though the medical experts expected her to survive for only two more *weeks*, Mary Alice lived for two more *years*.

Mother Teresa urged us all to slow down. She sensed that there was a great need for people to take time for each other. "Today we have no time even to look at each other, to talk to each other, to enjoy each other.... And so, less and less, we are in touch with each other. The world is lost for want of sweetness and kindness. People are starving for love because everybody is in such a great rush." She would add: "And so, let us always meet each other with a smile, for the smile is the beginning of love."

"It's Not a Sin to Be Rich"

God made the world rich enough to
feed and clothe every human being.
MOTHER TERESA

"It is not a sin to be rich," Mother Teresa taught us as we sat around her feet on the chapel floor; it is, in fact, a blessing. But wealth brings with it a great responsibility to share with others and help others with what we have been blessed with in our lives. It is not the wealth itself, but rather the avarice, greed, and selfishness that wealth can bring, which is a sin.

We are called to fill the world with the love and riches God has bestowed on us — not to keep everything for our own benefit. We must empty ourselves of all selfishness and greed to enable God to fill us with His love. "Riches, material or spiritual, can suffocate you if they are not used in the right way.... Remain as 'empty' as possible, so that God can fill you," she said.

There are individuals in this world who have an *overabundance* of material possessions, and there are countless others who have little or *nothing*. For a long time, I have felt that it would be such a beautiful thing if we could bridge the gap between excessive wealth and extreme poverty on earth. "The only thing that can remove poverty is sharing," Mother Teresa used to say. "God takes care of His poor people through us." There would be so much benefit to both sides, the rich and the poor alike, if we would come together and even things out so that every person in the world would have at least the basic necessities. Each one has so much to give the other. The rich have much to receive from coming into contact with Jesus "in His distressing disguise of the poor." The rewards are everlasting. The Missionaries of Charity serve as a bridge between those who are living in wealth and those who are dying in poverty. Mother herself had said, "Our task is to bring the rich and poor together, to be their point of contact." But she never wanted to force people to share their blessings; she would not allow anyone to do fundraising for her work; she wanted people to give out of love, never out of coercion.

"The world has enough for every man's need, but not enough for every man's greed," Mahatma Gandhi once said. Possessions are not meant to be hoarded. God has given us opportunities, gifts, and bless-ings so that we may cultivate them, and as Saint Francis de Sales said: "It is His will that we should make them useful and fruitful" for the good of all.

Mother Teresa taught that money is useful only if it serves to spread God's love. It can be used to feed the hungry — but people are hungry "not just for bread, but for love," for our presence, for our human contact. Something more than material things is needed, something more than food, clothing, and shelter. "There are evils that can't be remedied with money, only with love," she said. "The poor need our hands to serve them, they need our hearts to love them. Let us give, not from our abundance, but until it hurts." She wanted us not to be satis-fied with giving just money — she wanted us to reach out to others with love and compassion and understanding. And she wanted us to reap the rewards of doing so.

I felt that Mother Teresa had a holy attitude toward money. Her heart was set on the things of heaven and things that truly mattered. "Money — I don't think about it. It always comes. The Lord sends it. We do His work. He provides the means. If He does not give us the means, that shows that He does not want the work, so why worry?" Love, ser-vice, and spiritual things were far greater matters to her than finances. Her faith in God allowed her not to worry unduly about monetary and worldly things. "I don't want the work to become a business, but to remain a work of love," she insisted. "I want you to have that complete confidence that God won't let us down. Take Him at His Word and seek first the kingdom of heaven, and all else will be added on. Joy, peace, and unity are more important than money. If God wants me to do some-thing, He gives me the money" (*LOVE: A Fruit Always in Season*).

Once while I was visiting Mother Teresa, I wanted to give her as much as I could to help the Poorest of the Poor. I reached into my pocket and pulled out seven dollars. That was all I had. Feeling a little bit embarrassed that it was such a small amount, I gave it to her none-theless. She completely surprised me with her response. She held up the seven dollars in front of me, and looking directly into my eyes she said: "Do you know how many families this will feed?" I knew, then and there, that this humble offering would indeed feed not just a per-son, but many families. In Mother Teresa's hands, a little bit always went a long way. Even seven dollars could do so much good and produce a great yield when placed into the hands of a living saint!

Mother Teresa frequently pointed out that the spiritual poverty of the rich is much more serious than any material poverty of the poor — for spiritual things are everlasting, while material things pass away. It is our spiritual well-being that determines our eternal destiny. Our spirits are all that we can bring with us when we finish our journey on earth. It seems that those who are spiritually destitute, those who do not believe in God, are those who have not yet experienced the love and presence of God. Once a person feels the love of God, he believes. "God loves the world through us, you and me," Mother Teresa said. Through the presence of God within our souls, shining through our hands and hearts, all may come to believe. And through believing, all may come to everlasting life. It is really the eternal banquet in heaven that we should be striving to attain, not earthly ones which come to an end and only leave us hungry again. All the riches in the world cannot buy us eternal happiness. Jesus Christ Himself said: "Take heed, and beware of all covetousness; for a man's life does not consist in the abundance of his possessions" (Lk 12:15). We should be more concerned with growing rich in the sight of God than in growing rich in worldly things. "Here in America … you can easily be suffocated by things," Mother Teresa remarked. "And once you have them, you must give time to taking care of them. Then you have no time for each other or for the poor."

"One loses touch with God when one takes hold of money," she continued. "Once the longing for money comes, the longing also comes for what money can give: superfluous things, nice rooms, luxuries at the table, more clothes, fans, and so on. Our needs will increase, for one thing leads to another, and the result will be endless dissatisfaction." Her namesake, Saint Thérèse, said it this way: "Only that which is *eternal* can satisfy us."

Mother Teresa believed that "there must be a reason why some people can afford to live well. They must have worked for it. But I tell you … richness is given by God and it is our duty to divide it with those less favored." What is given to us by God as *blessings* in our life "is given to share, not to keep."

Seek to "live simply. Give example through simplicity," Mother Teresa taught by word and example, because "before God we are all poor."

The Fruits of This Experience in My Personal Life

As a student at Dartmouth, majoring in Economics, I had planned to get a good, high-paying job after graduation. I had planned to be "successful" in the traditional sense of the word. But after my trip to India, my heart was on fire with a very different dream. Rather than trying to make money for myself, I dreamed of making a difference for others. Rather than pursuing profits and prestige, I earnestly wanted to pursue God's will. Mother Teresa gave the expression "living the good life" a whole new meaning for me.

It is not possible to go to Calcutta, serve the Poorest of the Poor, witness Mother Teresa, and then come home the same. For me, poverty had taken on a human face, and I could not erase it from my mind. I could still practically feel the little orphaned children in my arms, and see their silent stares. It was no longer possible to live only for myself. The meaning of success had changed for me, and these beautiful words by Ralph Waldo Emerson became more precious:

> To laugh often and much; to win the respect of intelligent people and the affection of children; to earn the appreciation of honest critics, and endure the betrayal of false friends; to appreciate beauty; to find the best in others; to leave the world a little better place than you found it, whether by a healthy child, a garden patch, or a redeemed social condition; to know even one life breathed easier because you lived. This is to have succeeded.

During the initial weeks and months after I arrived home from India at the end of the summer, I felt that there was virtually nothing in this, my own world, which even vaguely resembled what I had seen and experienced in Calcutta. Since then, however, I have come to understand that it is all here as well as in Calcutta — the poverty, the suffering, the depth of meaning, the power of the human touch, and the incredible beauty. I have also come to realize that no matter where we go in this world, there are opportunities all around us to love and serve and make a difference in other people's lives.

I was very fortunate, upon graduation from college, to find employment here in the United States that seemed to fit with the work that I was doing in India with the young orphans and with the dying destitutes. I was offered a position at the Maine Children's Cancer Program, where I assisted in the care of children with cancer and their families. In too many cases, these were terminally ill children, and I felt so privileged to have been given the chance to know them and love them. It was a beautiful carry-over from what I had been doing in Calcutta.

This experience in India not only influenced my life's decisions as far as a career is concerned, but it also profoundly affected my spiritual development, my perception of the world, my appreciation of the blessings that God con-

A very happy graduation day at Dartmouth College with two of my closest college friends: Betsy Pelikan (center) and Susan Towler (right).

tinuously bestows on each one of us every day, my understanding of charity and true sanctity, my confidence and trust in God, my love for God, and my awareness of His constant kindness and infinite mercy toward us.

My Calcutta experience brought about many other lasting fruits as well:

- It resulted in a lasting relationship with Mother Teresa, who has been "a source of perpetual joy" in my life ever since I met her. This relationship with a living saint has brought me much inspiration and happiness over the years. Even if this were the *only* fruit of this journey to India, it would have been well worth the trip!

- As I was flying home from India at the end of the summer, I was keenly aware that I was taking away my "hands to serve and heart to love" the poor of Calcutta. I considered that there might be others whom I could send there to take my place. This dream came true very beautifully. Since I had established this contact with the Missionaries of Charity in India and New York and had created a special program for myself to volunteer with Mother Teresa's Order, I was able to hand on all of this information to the Tucker Foundation at Dartmouth — as well as to six other colleges and universities that participate in "The College Venture Program" headquartered at Brown University. Since 1986, a steady stream of volunteers has traveled from America to Calcutta to serve the Poorest of the Poor. At Dartmouth alone, it became one of the most popular off-campus programs offered by the Foundation.

- I continue to long for God's will in my life, not my own will, because I can see that His plans are much richer and more meaningful than my own. Even if God's plans include suffering and difficulties, they are far more desirable and fruitful than our own future plans. We have every reason to have total confidence in Him and to entrust our whole lives to Him.

- I continue to believe that *loving* one another is what life is all about. It is one of the greatest sources of happiness and fulfillment. In forgetting self, we find true joy and peace, and we find God. "This is the true reason for our existence," Mother Teresa said: "To be the sunshine of God's love."

- This experience has given me a strong and lasting desire to keep helping people. I have not been able to bring this desire to life in any extraordinary ways — only in simple ways, like bringing hot coffee and leftover fresh bread from local bakeries to homeless shelters and soup kitchens. My experience in Calcutta made me more sensitive to opportunities to serve. A friend of mine paid me a tremendous complement when she teasingly said that I had acquired "the Mother Teresa mentality!"

- It instilled in me a profound appreciation of the amazing power of prayer. It is life-giving and powerfully effective, when it is practiced with love, simplicity, and true faith. "Pray lovingly like children," Mother Teresa encouraged us all, "with an earnest desire to love much."

- The Holy Rosary and the Holy Eucharist are part of my daily life now. Before going to Calcutta, I seldom prayed the Rosary and I certainly did not understand the depth, richness, and power of meditating on the mysteries of it. I used to attend Mass on Sundays and Holy Days before going to India. Now I am eager to be nourished by the Bread of Life every day, and I feel that my day is incomplete if I have missed Holy Communion with Christ.

- It brought about a deeper awareness of God's Presence. Once you've tasted it, you thirst for it. He is so much closer to us than most of us realize. He is "the silent listener at every conversation...." God is with us, and we have every reason to be happy.

- I learned that we do not need to travel to a Third World country to find extreme poverty, suffering, hardship, disease, death, loneliness, or basic human needs. Neither do we have to look anywhere outside of ourselves to find the peace or the joy of giving and serving the poor. "No matter how tired I am," Mother Teresa said, "it's beautiful to bring a smile to someone's life. What greater joy can you have?" We do not have to look far away to find beauty, love, depth of meaning, and grace. It is all here. The capacity to love is within each one of us, and the need for love is all around us.

I cannot overemphasize that the whole purpose of life is to love. Mother Teresa said so beautifully that "God has created us for great things: to love and offer love...." Everything God does, everything He ever did, everything He will do, is for love. Created in His image and likeness, we are individually called to this same purpose. "Just allow people to see Jesus in you: to see how you pray, to see how you lead a pure life, to see how you deal with your family, to see how much peace there is in your family" she said. "Then you can look straight into their eyes and say: 'This is the way.' You speak from life, you speak from experience."

"We must live life beautifully; we have Jesus with us and He loves us," Mother Teresa said. "If we could only remember that God loves us, and we have an opportunity to love others as He loves us, not in big things, but in small things with great love, then [our country] becomes a nest of love ... a burning light of peace in the world...."

More Marvelous "Fruits"

This book would be far too lengthy if I were to write about *all* of the wonderful consequences of meeting Mother Teresa. I will highlight one story as an example of how lives have been touched. I refer to it as the "miracle baby" story.

I gave a slide presentation about my experience in Calcutta to a group of people in Maine some years ago. There was a newspaper editor in the audience who subsequently wrote an article for the *Church World*. On Thursday, July 23, 1992, the paper published an article on the front cover with a large photograph of my drawing of a child in the palm of God's Hand (which Mother Teresa had asked me to draw, and upon which Mother Teresa had written). On exactly that same day, a little baby was born prematurely at Maine Medical Center in Portland. Her name was Emily. She was only twenty-nine weeks and she weighed only two pounds, one ounce. She was so tiny that her father could literally hold this baby *in the palm of his hand*. It was an intense time of concern for this father and his family, because his wife and newborn baby's conditions grew progressively worse. By the end of the first day, little Emily's weight dropped to less than one pound; yet the doctors were even more concerned about her mother, saying: "If only the mother would do as well as the baby." Neither one was expected to survive the crisis. "The worst part," the father said, "was when they said they were doing everything they could. There was nothing more they could do." One doctor suggested that he contact a priest. When the priest failed to arrive, Rick, the father, felt that he had been abandoned by God.

On the same day that this little one was born, Emily's great, great aunt Gert was the first to see the article, which had appeared in the paper with my illustration of the child in God's Hand. She was stunned. She says there were no words to describe what she felt. She "just couldn't put it down." The picture gave the family strength and hope. The timing of it was perhaps what made the biggest impression. The baby's father, Rick, kept picking it up and looking at it. He said "I could hold Emily in the palm of my hand — and look at that little baby!" For Rick, even more than the drawing itself, it was the words written next to the drawing that "said it all." It was as if God was telling him that he wasn't alone. *See, "I shall not forget you"* (Is 49:15). He knew, upon seeing that picture, that God had not abandoned him in his most difficult of times.

Although the baby's mother, Mary Jo, was expected to have serious kidney and liver problems for the rest of her life, if she survived, she is not only alive today, but in amazingly good health. She does not have any of the problems that the doctors had expected. And little Emily is full of vitality — a pure joy! She is a charming and lovable little girl with a personality like a firecracker! She is just bursting with love and happiness. Her family refers to her as their "miracle baby." They actually believe that two miracles took place, because two lives were saved. It was an amazing coincidence that the premature birth of this baby took place on the exact date that this article was published, giving comfort and peace to Emily's family. Mother Teresa played a beautiful role in this story by treasuring God's Word and inviting me to make the drawing in the first place. The family played a leading role by having faith in God's infinite mercy and by cherishing their baby and each other. The doctors and nurses involved were exemplary. The rest took place by the pure grace of God.

At the time of this extraordinary unfolding of events, Rick wanted Mother Teresa to know that "her work extends far beyond what she thinks it does."

The Little Flower Had a Tremendous Influence on Mother Teresa

This book would not be complete if I failed to discuss more fully Saint Thérèse of Lisieux, the "Little Flower," who has touched the lives of both Mother Teresa and me in very rich and beautiful ways. Coming to know her is one of the many precious fruits of this experience with Mother Teresa.

Bishop Patrick Ahern of New York said Mother Teresa "was fond of pointing out that she took her religious name not from the great Saint Teresa of Ávila but from the Little Thérèse of Lisieux, for whom she had unbounded admiration."[64] Mother Teresa herself confessed: "We all want to love God, but how? The Little Flower is a most wonderful example. She did small things with great love. Ordinary things with extraordinary love. That is why she became a great saint." And that is one of the reasons why Mother Teresa became a great saint. She followed the Little Flower's teachings so beautifully.

"Little Thérèse," as she wished to be called, was a beautiful young woman from France who entered a Carmelite Monastery in her hometown of Lisieux at the age of fifteen. She lived a cloistered religious life behind those convent walls for only nine years, until her life ended at

St. Thérèse of Lisieux.

age twenty-four. For this reason and others, in our hearts, she is forever young! She has had a lasting influence on millions of lives throughout the world, in spite of the fact that she was hardly even known during her short life. Saint Thérèse was incredibly young when she died, yet she had attained such *wisdom*, such a degree of *love*, and such *sanctity* that she has been hailed as "the greatest saint of modern times." In 1997, Pope John Paul II solemnly declared Saint Thérèse the thirty-third Doctor of the Church — only the third woman to be given this title in the two-thousand-year history of the Church. Thérèse, by far, is the youngest person to receive this highly prestigious honor. Before she left this world, Saint Thérèse herself affirmed: "I will spend my heaven doing good on earth," and anyone who knows her knows that indeed she has been doing just that.

I wrote to Mother Teresa, just a month before her life ended in 1997, about the exciting news that Saint Thérèse was going to be declared a Doctor of the Church: "It is truly amazing that a little soul who was so hidden and unknown during her brief life on earth is so known and loved by so many people throughout the world and is being lifted to such heights! God's ways are so wonderful!" When Mother discovered this news about Saint Thérèse being declared a Doctor, she exclaimed: "Oh very nice! I'm also Teresa!"

It was through Mother Teresa that I was "introduced" to Saint Thérèse of Lisieux in two ways. First, I had learned who inspired Mother Teresa to choose her religious name: "Not the big Saint Teresa of Ávila, but the *little* one," she used to say. I always treasured that information in my heart, even though I knew absolutely nothing about this "Little" Thérèse. In 1987, that all changed. While I was living for two weeks in Mother Teresa's convent in New York, at Mother's request, I read for the first time a book about the Little Flower. It was entitled *The Complete Spiritual Doctrine of Saint Thérèse of Lisieux*, and I could hardly put it down. I was absolutely enraptured by what I was learning about the Little Flower. Knowing that Little Thérèse was especially dear to Mother Teresa, I was very eager to learn who she was. I also listened with great fervor to every word of a spiritual lecture given to us by an elderly and saintly priest during that two-week visit. I soaked up every word he said about Saint Thérèse like a little flower thirsting for water! Ever since then, after coming to know Saint Thérèse, I have felt an affinity with her. It is as if she has been with me ever since, helping me and bringing beautiful blessings into my life.

I find it interesting to note that my two-week visit at Mother Teresa's convent in New York, during which I "met" Saint Thérèse for the first time, happened to take place at the time when the Missionaries of Charity were celebrating the combined Feast Days of both Mother Teresa *and* Saint Thérèse, on October 1. This coincidence had powerful meaning. There could not have been a more appropriate occasion for me to meet the Little Flower through Mother Teresa's intercession.

Saint Thérèse has been both the intercessor and the focus of the work I have undertaken in recent years. I have been given opportunities to translate books from French into English, and to have them published here in the United States by various publishers. Interestingly enough, each one of these books has been about Saint Thérèse of Lisieux. When I learned about the subject matter of each translation project — namely, Saint Thérèse — I felt like saying to the editors: "Do you realize who it is that you are offering this opportunity to? I happen to *love* Saint Thérèse!"[65] Each project, I felt, was a tremendous honor and a true labor of love. It has been a very special part of my life's work, and it would not have come to be had I not met Mother Teresa.[66]

A friend of mine asked me how I came upon these translation opportunities and, more importantly, how I came to know about Saint Thérèse in the first place. As soon as my friend learned that it was through Mother Teresa that I had come to know the Little Flower, and it was in turn through my love for Thérèse that I had come across these wonderful opportunities to translate books, she asked me, "Did you ever tell Mother Teresa this?" I was embarrassed to say I had not. In the ten years since Mother Teresa first introduced me to the Little Flower, I had never thought to turn around and acknowledge what a great blessing this had been to me. On that very day, I promised my friend that I would go home and write a letter of acknowledgement. In what proved to be one of my very last letters to Mother Teresa, I poured out my heart in thanksgiving to her for bringing Saint Thérèse into my life, and I glued a little flower to the end of the letter.

I imagine that many of the letters that Mother Teresa received contained requests for her prayers, requests for her to speak at various places, requests for religious articles, etc. I did not ask Mother Teresa for anything. I simply told her what a difference she had made in my life. This letter, written in early May 1997, apparently meant something to Mother Teresa. She ended up carrying it with her all the way across the world — from India, to Italy, to America. She received it in Calcutta just before departing on one of her final missions, and had it with her in Rome when she visited with Pope John Paul II for the last time. She was in Rome when she wrote her response to me on the back of a piece of paper with a picture of herself holding a small child with the words "See! I will not forget you…." Mother Teresa was grateful that the Little Flower has been such a source of inspiration for me. "She will help you on the path of holiness," she wrote. At the end of her letter, she said, "I am praying for you." Instead of mailing her letter to me from Rome, however, she carried it with her to the South Bronx. Her letter was postmarked from New York. When I see photographs of Mother Teresa with Our Holy Father during their last earthly visit, I delight in believing that my written outpouring of gratitude was actually *with* her at that time!

Mother Teresa and Saint Thérèse had a lot in common, I believe. They were spiritual sisters. Mother Teresa's life and spirit were marked by a beautiful simplicity. Her words, her ways and her love were simple. Likewise, Little Thérèse had been told by her subprioress at one time: "…your soul is extremely simple, but when you will be perfect, you will be even more simple; the closer one approaches to God, the simpler one becomes."

Their two lives complemented each other beautifully. One lived in silence and solitude behind the veil of a cloister wall, while the other was quite visible on the world stage. Mother Teresa traveled across the whole earth carrying God's love, peace, and light of truth to the Poorest of the Poor and to millions of others. Saint Thérèse, having entered a Carmelite Monastery in the same village where she was raised, and having remained there until her early death, was hidden and obscure; no one even knew what to say about her in her obituary when she died. Yet, her heart was on fire to be a missionary, to travel to the most distant corners of the world, and to save countless souls. She prayed: "But *Oh my Beloved*, one mission alone would not be sufficient for me. I would want to preach the Gospel on all the five continents simultaneously and even to the most remote isles. I would be a missionary, not for a few years only, but from the beginning of creation until the consummation of the ages."[67] Because of her immense desires and in spite of the fact that she lived within a strictly cloistered monastery, Saint Thérèse was named the patroness of missionaries. The hearts of these two saints burned with the same desires and the same fire — love for God and love for souls.

When Little Thérèse was in her final agony, wasted away by tuberculosis, her final words were: "My God, I love You!" Similarly, at the last moments of her life, Mother Teresa had a prayer on her lips and Our Lord in her mind as she kept repeating the Holy Name of "Jesus, Jesus, Jesus."

I find it fascinating that the Little Flower was called home to God in September 1897, and that Mother Teresa was called home in September 1997, exactly 100 years later.

Chapter Nine

Mother Teresa's Going Home to God

Angels don't remain on earth once they've fulfilled God's will,
for they return immediately to Him.
SAINT THÉRÈSE

In 1987, someone asked me what would happen when Mother Teresa died. This question took me totally by surprise because in my mind, I knew Mother Teresa would never die! I was quite convinced of this. I had just been in her presence not too long before and the thought of Mother's spirit expiring was unimaginable. Wisdom, grace, and truth are eternal, and love *never ends*. Mother Teresa's soul was filled with all these things. She would never pass away. I could more easily picture Mother Teresa ascending into heaven than I could picture her dying. In a very powerful and beautiful way, she was more spiritual than physical, and that which is of the spirit lasts forever. The essence of Mother Teresa, her spiritual being, would live on eternally. Rarely does God favor a soul with such a grace as ascending into heaven. The only ones I know of who were favored in that way were Jesus Christ Himself, the great prophet Elijah, and the Blessed Virgin Mary, who was taken, body and soul, into heaven. For the first time in my life, I could deeply understand Christ's Ascension. I could understand how such an extraordinary thing was possible, because I had stood in the presence of Mother Teresa.

In 1981, Mother Teresa and Sister Priscilla visited a doctor. He informed each of them separately that Mother had a bad heart condition and that she must rest and take care of herself. Mother Teresa did not want anyone to know. Sister Priscilla recalled that Mother, "Went right on doing whatever she had to do, keeping all the engagements, living the life to the full.... At times people don't seem to realize that she is human and the demands on her are very great. We seem to think that she has this energy which just never gets used up." Mother Teresa kept a busy schedule, in spite of the doctor's advice, and she would say, "I feel Jesus is asking this of me — and I have never said 'no' to Jesus." In the words of Sister Priscilla, "Mother said she wanted to die on her feet and I think that's just what she's doing — giving herself to the last drop."

Mother Teresa was admitted to a hospital in Calcutta with malaria about a year before she died. She had suffered cardiac arrest and her condition began deteriorating rapidly. She was put on a respirator after her heart stopped beating for about a minute. The world held its breath. Cardinal James Hickey of Washington issued a statement calling for the American people to pray for Mother Teresa: "Just as Mother Teresa has opened her heart to the sick and the dying, so now we open our hearts to her in prayer."

A week before this happened, before news of her hospitalization spread, I was eager to thank Mother Teresa for a special letter that I had

I always found it interesting that of all things, Mother Teresa was told that she had a weak heart when, in every other sense, besides the physical one, her heart was so great and strong! She had been told by her doctors for a long time that she must slow down, get more rest, take her medications, etc., but she kept going. And she kept offering up her pain to God for the good of souls. She maintained a grueling schedule right up until the last weeks of her life, traveling across the world from India to Europe to America on various missions. Sister Luke (the Sister Superior of the Home for the Dying, shown here with Mother Teresa) said: "Until her last breath, she'll be on her feet, working."

just received from her, so I sent a bouquet of red roses to her Mother-house in Calcutta with my love and prayers for her. The flowers were scheduled to arrive on August 22. I had no idea at the time I ordered this bouquet that Mother Teresa would be in critical condition at the time of their delivery in Calcutta. Early in the morning, on August 24, I was wondering if my flowers had arrived safely at Mother Teresa's house. I picked up our local morning paper and was amazed by what I saw. There was a photograph of Mother Teresa's Sisters praying for Mother in the convent chapel in Calcutta on August 23, and there in front of the altar was one big bouquet of roses!

Mother Teresa passed away on September 5, 1997 at the Mother-house of the Missionaries of Charity in Calcutta, ten days after her 87th birthday (August 26). Sister Gertrude told me that Mother Teresa had been praying much that day, and suddenly she began having diffi-culty breathing. She needed oxygen, but within moments of having an oxygen machine brought to her, there was a power outage in Calcutta! The machine was completely useless. As the seconds turned into min-utes, Sister Gertrude was privileged to be there with Mother Teresa, holding her and caring for her as she breathed her last. I met Sister Gertrude in Rome in October 1997, just weeks after Mother passed away. Sister told me that she still speaks to Mother Teresa often, asking for prayers and affectionately expressing her love for Mother. As I lis-tened to Sister Gertrude's account of Mother Teresa's final days and minutes on earth, I could not hold back my tears.

Sister Nirmala wrote in November of 1997: "…Jesus opened His Heart and took Mother in so quickly that the world had no chance to pray and hold Mother back. He really came like a thief in the night. Yes, on that night, the whole of Calcutta went into darkness as the electricity failed. And Jesus stole Mother away, so fast, so quietly!… Let us prepare our hearts so that anytime He comes, He may find us ready, as Mother was, to go home with Him." Even now, from heaven, "Mother is as busy as ever obtaining graces for us from the Heart of Jesus," Sister Nirmala added. Mother continues to have great love for us and for our spiritual growth. Sister Nirmala urged us all to have "a loving and fervent response in living out Mother's wishes" for us.

During the years leading up to Mother Teresa's last days, as we heard news that she was hospitalized and in critical condition, I could

Sister Gertrude was the second woman to join Mother Teresa's Order, back in 1949. When she approached Mother to ask to become a member of the Missionaries of Charity, Mother welcomed her happily and wrote: "Great day — Magdalene (now Sister Gertrude) joined the little Society. She is a fine strong soul." Apparently Mother Teresa had told her, "I want you to study medicine," and even though Sister Gertrude had no desire to do so, she obeyed. I am sure that this Sister never dreamed, almost fifty years ago, that one day, precisely *because* of her medical training, she would be the one holding and caring for this blessed saint during the last moments of her life.

not bear to let her go. Today's world is in such great need of saints and we could not afford to lose this one. But when the time came for God to call her home to heaven, I felt a great peace. I even felt joy at knowing where she was and what comfort and happiness she was experiencing. She had served God and others so tirelessly, and now she could finally *rest* a little bit!

I pray that there will always be saints like Mother Teresa in the world. She was a great beacon of light and a model of goodness. She left us a beautifully inspiring legacy of love and faith. And she lives on, not only in heaven, but also in so many hearts all over the world. The work of love that she was doing on earth will certainly continue, because, as she always reminded us: "The work is God's work, and He will see to it." But it is up to us now to be carriers of this same light of love and truth. Now it is our turn.

There is not a living soul on earth who does not have the power to love.

In a letter to her co-workers, Mother Teresa wrote she knew her life's work was "a living miracle of the love of God ... in action. God has shown His greatness by using nothingness — so let us always remain in our nothingness — so as to give God a free hand to use us without consulting us. Let us accept whatever He gives and give whatever He takes with a big smile.... My heart is filled with joy and expectation of the beautiful things God will do through each one of you. Beautiful are the ways of God if we allow Him to use us as He wants."

The very last time I stood in Mother Teresa's presence was just weeks before she died. She was in Washington, D.C., in June 1997 to receive the Congressional Gold Medal. She also attended a special Mass in which several Missionaries of Charity took their religious vows in New York. I traveled by bus from Maine to Manhattan, took the subway to Harlem, and even ran a few blocks by foot to catch a van heading to the South Bronx to attend the ceremony at Saint Anthony's Church. I knew that Mother Teresa was going to be there, and I had an endless desire to see her "one last time." Even though I had to travel by bus, subway, van, and foot to see her — it was well worth the effort. This time, it truly was my last time.

It was astounding that even in her weakened condition, Mother Teresa was still willing to give every drop of herself to others. Understanding that the vast majority of us were there out of love for her and love for God, she was willing to reach out to every single person who had entered the church that day. She was seated in a wheelchair, and she greeted each one of us, *hundreds* of us, giving each of us Miraculous Medals. Her head was bowed down and her face was lowered; her voice was weaker and softer than I had ever heard it before. I silently kissed her hand as I received her gift of medals and her blessings. My heart was dying to say something to her, to tell her who I was, to speak again with her. But I did not speak, nothing more than "God bless you, Mother! God bless you," as I *left* her — for I could see how weak she was and I did not want to make her raise her head or hold up the line of people. I was filled with pity and gratitude to see how much it took for her to stay there in that wheelchair for all those hours, greeting each person with a blessing.

Photo by James Baca, CNS

"Precious in the sight of the Lord is the death of his saints" (Ps 116:15). As Mother Teresa taught in such a comforting and pacifying way, death is not the end of life, it is only a change. It is really a beginning. In Mother's own words, "The heart and the soul live forever. . . . Death is nothing but going home to God."

During the seven-hour bus ride home to Maine that same day, I wished so deeply that I had told her one more thing: "I love you, Mother Teresa." I wanted so much for her to know this! And so I wrote a letter to her, with this final outpouring from my heart. "I always want to tell you that I love you," I shared. And I knew that she received my message, because she responded to it personally.

Like my own mother at home, Mother Teresa has been a beautiful example to me. A model of humility, which is one of my favorite virtues of all. From humility come so many other virtues, because God can easily fill what is empty and humble. If I tried to tell Mother Teresa, in writing, everything she had taught me and all that she meant to me, I would never finish my letter. My "thank you" was always so little compared to what she had given me.

Mother Teresa's response to my letter came to me on August 18, 1997, less than three weeks before she passed away. My great joy in reading it came from knowing that she had received what I had longed to tell her. Mother Teresa has made an extraordinary difference in my life. Her inspiration, guidance, and lessons have brought me to where I am today. They have indeed re-directed the course of my life. My plans, before meeting her, had been good ones — they certainly were not bad, anyway — but my experience with Mother Teresa taught me that there is more to life than the comfort and enjoyment of visible things. There is more to life than just taking care of ourselves. There is a whole other world, not only a world of suffering and poverty, but also a world of invisible things: the spiritual life. She taught me that the secret to true happiness and to a deep sense of fulfillment in life has more to do with spiritual things than with material things.

"Keep on praying for us," Mother Teresa wrote to me, "that we may continue God's work with great love, that our lives remain woven with Jesus in the Eucharist and that we put the oneness with Jesus in action to the service of the Poorest of the Poor."

Mother Teresa's last letter to her Sisters, Brothers, volunteers — to us *all* really — was dated September 5, 1997, the *very same day* she made her most important journey, her journey to heaven. "My dearest Children," she wrote:

> This brings you Mother's love, prayer, and blessing that each one of you may be only all for Jesus through Mary. I know that Mother says often — "Be only all for Jesus through Mary" — but that is because that is all Mother wants for you, all Mother wants from you. If in your heart you are only all for Jesus through Mary, and if you do everything only all for Jesus through Mary, you will be a true M.C. (Missionary of Charity).
>
> Thank you for all the loving wishes you sent for Society Feast [September 10, Inspiration Day]. We have much to thank God for, especially that He has given us Our Lady's spirit to be the spirit of our Society. *Loving Trust* and *Total Surrender* made Our Lady say "Yes" to the message of the angel, and *Cheerfulness* made her run in haste to serve her cousin Elizabeth. That is so much our life — saying "Yes" to Jesus and running in haste to serve Him in the Poorest of the Poor. Let us keep very close to Our Lady and she will make that same spirit grow in each one of us [emphasis added].
>
> September 10th is coming very close. That is another beautiful chance for us to stand near Our Lady, to listen to the Thirst of Jesus and to answer with our whole heart. It is only with Our Lady that we can hear Jesus cry: "I Thirst," and it is only with Our Lady that we can thank God properly for giving this great gift to our Society. Last year was the Golden Jubilee of Inspira-

tion Day, and I hope that the whole year has been one of thanksgiving. We will never come to the end of the gift that came to Mother for the Society on that day, and so we must never stop thanking God for it. Let our gratitude be our strong resolution to quench the Thirst of Jesus by lives of real charity — love for Jesus in prayer, love for Jesus in our Sisters, love for Jesus in the Poorest of the Poor — nothing else.

And now I have heard that Jesus is giving us one more gift. This year, one hundred years after she went home to Jesus, Holy Father is declaring the Little Flower (Saint Thérèse of Lisieux) to be a Doctor of the Church. Can you imagine — for doing little things with great love the Church is making her a Doctor, like Saint Augustine and the big Saint Teresa! It is just like Jesus said in the Gospel to the one who was seated in the lowest place: "Friend, come up higher." So let us *keep very small* and follow the Little Flower's way of *trust* and *love* and *joy,* and we will fulfill Mother's promise to give saints to Mother Church [emphasis added].

Mother Teresa's successor, Sister Nirmala, finished Mother's letter, writing: "This is the last letter of our Mother which was ready for her signature. But Jesus came to take away our beloved Mother so suddenly that it remained unsigned. I am sending this to you with great love. This is our Mother's last message to us. Let us take it to our hearts."

"Sometimes our light goes out, but it is blown again into flame by an encounter with another human being; each of us owes deepest thanks to those who have rekindled this inner light." These beautiful words by Albert Schweitzer always fill my heart with gratitude to Mother Teresa of Calcutta.

I love you, Mother Teresa.
You are still right here
in my heart.

Acknowledgments

❧

My heartfelt appreciation goes out to a large family of wonderful people.

First, I am eternally grateful to **Mother Teresa** herself. She has been so good to me from the start. This personal written testimony would never have existed if Mother Teresa had not given it her blessing and approval. Mother went so far as to allow me to share all her words and lessons freely with everyone — with her usual greatness of heart.

Also at the top of my list of wonderful people to thank is **Bishop Patrick Ahern** of New York, who has been a channel of grace, guidance, and generous support every step of the way. His inspiring words and enthusiasm for this new literary endeavor have brought tears of joy to my eyes and true courage to my heart.

I am greatly indebted to **Nicholas Forstmann** for his generous sponsorship of this entire effort. He believed in this book project as being worthy of his support, and I pray that in heaven he can now see the fullness of my inexpressible gratitude.

Also, I wish to thank my beloved aunt **Elizabeth Conroy** and my uncle **Joseph P. Conroy**. Their loving contribution has enabled us to include so many of the beautiful photographs in this book. They wrote to me: "Dear Susan: It is our joy to help Mother Teresa, God's messenger — and you, her herald. People are starving for her message of love." Thank you so much, Uncle Joe and Aunt Ibby.

I also cannot adequately express my appreciation to **Angela Cox**. Every time she touched this book project, she managed to bring about little miracles. Her insights, editing, and every ounce of her assistance have been a blessing.

Very special thanks are due to **John D'Angelo** for his meticulous editing of my manuscript. John put remarkable honesty, sensitivity, and efficiency into this task, and I wonder what I would have done without him.

My heartfelt thanks goes out to everyone at *Our Sunday Visitor*, especially **Lisa Grote,** the Project Editor who truly does have an angel on her shoulder guiding her pen, and **Jacqueline Lindsey**, the Managing Editor, whose beautiful words of encouragement and great personal efforts brought this book to life. From the start, Jackie lifted my heart into the clouds every time she expressed her expectations concerning this book!

I feel endless gratitude to *every* member of my family for their loving support and enthusiasm as I set out to write this story. "Honorable mention" goes to my brother **David** and his wife **Julie Conroy,** who were tireless in advising me, editing my work, and showing an unwavering faith that I could actually fulfill this mission. My sister, **Helen Conroy**, shared her professional expertise in helping me to seek formal permission to reprint some indispensable material for this book. My brothers **Jamie** and **Brian Conroy** came to my assistance every time I encountered computer challenges and technical difficulties; they turned major roadblocks into little speed bumps. And my beloved parents, **Ruth** and **Francis Conroy**, inspired me with their "complete confidence" that this labor of love would one day bear this fruit.

So many people encouraged and supported me in beautiful ways — **Father John Scahill** *insisted* on helping me recover my lost manuscript when my computer crashed at a very inopportune time; **Jane Franchetti** reached out with a financial gift to help me get started; **Henry Gosselin** graciously offered to review my work and make recommendations; **Craig Denekas** offered excellent advice and guidance as I tried to navigate my way through the book contract; **Father James Nadeau** at the Cathedral of the Immaculate Conception in Portland, Maine, unhesitatingly offered to facilitate my contact with various photographers and publishers overseas — a very unexpected and generous gift to me; **Mary Ibrahim** actually relayed these important international communications on my behalf.

I send out a warm embrace of appreciation to my friends who shared their wonderful photographs of Mother Teresa and her work in India: **Bruce Aguilar, Paul Amberg, Irene Chasse, Jane Clement, Paul Hulewicz,** and **Ray and Lauretta Seabeck.** I also wish to express special thanks to **Bob Roller** at Catholic News Service for his excellent assistance in selecting photographs.

Special honor is due to the renown artist **Ted Lewin** for his stunning illustration of Mother Teresa that was published in *Family Circle* magazine in April 1980. My mother sent me the page from the magazine and I carried it with me all the way to Calcutta. I will never forget Mother Teresa's reaction to seeing the picture, which she signed and which I still hold close to my heart. Thank you, Mr. Lewin, for allowing me to share your beautiful work.

Very special thanks are also due to the award-winning film producers, **Ann** and **Jeanette Petrie**, for graciously allowing me to share some of Mother Teresa's lessons of love and holiness from their documentary film *Mother Teresa*. They have been so honorable and loyal in protecting yet sharing our beloved friend's teachings.

From the depths of my heart I thank the **Missionaries of Charity** for the gift of their prayers, contributions, and ongoing inspiration. In particular I must mention **Sister Priscilla,** at the Motherhouse in Calcutta, India, who granted me full permission to share all the priceless spiritual teachings in this book. She further granted worldwide rights to publish this material in all languages and in all editions. I am so happily indebted to her!

I reach out with sincere gratitude to **Father Conrad DeMeester** of Belgium for his many words of wisdom that have graced the pages of this book and for his endless *power of confidence* that this work of love would one day blossom.

To this day, I am gratefully remembering the **UNUM Life Insurance Company employees** who went out of their way to provide feedback to me after seeing my Calcutta slide presentation back in 1996. Their words inspired me to seek personal approval from Mother Teresa to share my Calcutta experience in the form of a book. What a difference they have made! You are now holding the fruit of their thoughtfulness in your hands.

Endnotes

❧

[1] *Life in the Spirit* (Reflections, Meditations, Prayers), *The Love of Christ* (Spiritual Counsels), and *A Gift for God* (Prayers and Meditations), published by Harper & Row.

[2] From the beautiful documentary film *Mother Teresa*, by the award-winning producers Ann and Jeanette Petrie, narrated by Sir Richard Attenborough. Copyright 1986, Petrie Productions, Inc.

[3] Ibid.

[4] Ibid.

[5] I hope that he receives many graces for his kindness to me. I also hope that someday he may read this book so that he will know I am still remembering him with grateful affection.

[6] Rai, Raghu and Navin Chawla. *Faith and Compassion — The Life and Work of Mother Teresa*. Element Books, 1996.

[7] *Women's Day* magazine. A Selection of Mother Teresa's moving and inspirational words. Dec. 19, 1989.

[8] Moorhouse, Geoffrey. *Calcutta*. Hold, Rinehart & Winston, 1971.

[9] Tower, Courtney, "Mother Teresa's Work of Grace," *Reader's Digest*, December, 1987.

[10] Doig, Desmond. *Mother Teresa: Her People and Her Work*. Fount Paperbacks, 1978. © Nachiketa Publications, 1976.

[11] Goodwin, Jan, "A Week With Mother Teresa," *Ladies Home Journal*, May 1984.

[12] Cunningham, Frank, editor. *Words to Love By*. Based on interviews by Michael Nabicht and Gaynell Cronin. Ave Maria Press, 1983.

[13] Long white religious garments. Saris are worn traditionally by Hindu women, consisting of lightweight cloth with one end wrapped around the waist to form a long skirt and the other draped over the shoulder or covering the head.

[14] From the documentary film *Mother Teresa*, by Ann and Jeanette Petrie.

[15] On the night before His Crucifixion, at the Last Supper, Jesus took bread into His Sacred Hands, gave thanks and praise to His heavenly Father, broke the bread, gave it to His disciples and said: "This is my body which is given for you. Do this in remembrance of me" (Lk 22:19). At Our Lord's Word, and through the words of His consecrated priests, ordinary bread is transubstantiated into the actual Body of Christ. Every Mass fulfills what Our Lord commanded us to do at the Last Supper, and it "commemorates" Him, makes Him present to us.

[16] Tower, Courtney, "Mother Teresa's Work of Grace," *Reader's Digest*, December, 1987.

[17] This is a Catholic tradition that Mother Teresa embraced and cherished. We kneel in adoration of the Sacred Body of Christ in the Blessed Sacrament, for

the Lord Jesus had said: "For this is the will of my Father, that every one who sees the Son and believes in him should have eternal life; and I will raise him up at the last day" (Jn 6:40).

[18] Cunningham, Frank, editor. *Words to Love By.* Based on interviews by Michael Nabicht and Gaynell Cronin. Ave Maria Press, 1983.

[19] Ibid.

[20] Hunt, Dorothy, editor. *LOVE: A Fruit Always in Season.* Ignatius Press, 1987.

[21] Spink, Kathyrn. *Life in the Spirit: Reflections, Meditations, Prayers.* Harper & Row, 1983.

[22] Mother Teresa. *The Love of Christ: Spiritual Counsels.* Harper & Row, 1992.

[23] Other special prayers that Mother Teresa taught and prayed include "Radiating Christ," "Dearest Lord, the Great Healer," "Oh Mary, Mother of Jesus, give me your Heart," and "Immaculate Heart of Mary, cause of our joy…" which are located in later chapters of this book.

[24] Gonzalez-Balado, José Luis. *Stories of Mother Teresa: Her Smile and Her Words.* Liguori Publications, 1983.

[25] From the prayer "Radiating Christ," which we prayed with Mother Teresa every day.

[26] Spink, Kathyrn. *Life in the Spirit: Reflections, Meditations, Prayers.* Harper & Row, 1983.

[27] Mother Teresa: *A Gift for God: Prayers and Meditations.* Harper & Row, 1975.

[28] Hunt, Dorothy, editor. *LOVE: A Fruit Always in Season.* Ignatius Press, 1987.

[29] Serrou, Robert. *Teresa of Calcutta: A Pictorial Biography.* McGraw Hill Book Company, 1980.

[30] Acts 20:35.

[31] LeJoly, Edward, S.J. *Mother Teresa of Calcutta: A Biography.* Harper & Row, 1977, 1983.

[32] Gonzalez-Balado, José Luis, editor and Janet N. Playfoot. *My Life for the Poor.* Harper & Row, 1985.

[33] Cunningham, Frank, editor. *Words to Love By.* Based on interviews by Michael Nabicht and Gaynell Cronin. Ave Maria Press, 1983.

[34] From the documentary film *Mother Teresa,* by Ann and Jeanette Petrie.

[35] Tower, Courtney, "Mother Teresa's Work of Grace," *Reader's Digest,* December 1987.

[36] *Time* magazine. "Seeker of Souls." September 15, 1997.

[37] Tower, Courtney, "Mother Teresa's Work of Grace," *Reader's Digest,* December 1987.

[38] Mother Teresa. *The Love of Christ: Spiritual Counsels.* Harper & Row, 1992.

[39] Gonzalez-Balado, José Luis. *In My Own Words.* Liguori Publications, 1996.

[40] Saint Thérèse of Lisieux. *Story of a Soul.* ICS Publications, 1975, 1976.

[41] Hunt, Dorothy, editor. *LOVE: A Fruit Always in Season.* Ignatius Press, 1987.

[42] Spink, Kathyrn. *Life in the Spirit: Reflections, Meditations, Prayers*. Harper & Row, 1983.

[43] Ibid.

[44] Cunningham, Frank, editor. *Words to Love By*. Based on interviews by Michael Nabicht and Gaynell Cronin. Ave Maria Press, 1983.

[45] Hunt, Dorothy, editor. *LOVE: A Fruit Always in Season*. Ignatius Press, 1987.

[46] Rai, Raghu and Navin Chawla. *Faith and Compassion — The Life and Work of Mother Teresa*. Element Books, 1996.

[47] Ibid.

[48] Ibid.

[49] Gonzalez-Balado, José Luis, editor and Janet N. Playfoot. *My Life for the Poor*. Harper & Row, 1985.

[50] Saint Thérèse of Lisieux.

[51] From the documentary film *Mother Teresa*, by Ann and Jeanette Petrie.

[52] Gonzales-Balado, José Luis, editor and Janet N. Playfoot. *My Life for the Poor*. Harper & Row, 1985.

[53] Saint Thérèse of Lisieux.

[54] Cunningham, Frank, editor. *Words to Love By*. Based on interviews by Michael Nabicht and Gaynell Cronin. Ave Maria Press, 1983.

[55] Mother Teresa. *The Love of Christ: Spiritual Counsels*. Harper & Row, 1992.

[56] Cunningham, Frank, editor. *Words to Love By*. Based on interviews by Michael Nabicht and Gaynell Cronin. Ave Maria Press, 1983.

[57] From the documentary film *Mother Teresa*, by Ann and Jeanette Petrie.

[58] Hunt, Dorothy, editor. *LOVE: A Fruit Always in Season*. Ignatius Press, 1987.

[59] *Columbia* magazine. "Remembering Mother Teresa." November 1997.

[60] Cunningham, Frank, editor. *Words to Love By*. Based on interviews by Michael Nabicht and Gaynell Cronin. Ave Maria Press, 1983.

[61] *Time* magazine. "Seeker of Souls." September 15, 1997.

[62] Hunt, Dorothy, editor. *LOVE: A Fruit Always in Season*. Ignatius Press, 1987.

[63] Mother Teresa. *The Love of Christ: Spiritual Counsels*. Harper & Row, 1992.

[64] Ahern, Bishop Patrick V. *Story of a Love*. Doubleday, 1998.

[65] The first book, on which I worked with a team of translators, is entitled *Saint Thérèse of Lisieux: Her Life, Times and Teachings*. The second one, on which I worked as the sole translator, is *The Power of Confidence*. I recently finished a third translation project for a publisher in France; it is a booklet entitled "I offer myself to Your Love, "which is about Saint Thérèse's offering of herself to God's merciful love.

[66] Most recently, I was invited to translate the final piece of Saint Thérèse's writings, which has not been published in English (the work is more than 100 years old). Her recreational plays, written for her religious community to perform, will soon be available in the United States for the first time, through ICS Publications of Washington, D.C.

[67] Saint Thérèse of Lisieux. *Story of a Soul*. ICS Publications, 1975, 1976.

Sources

Mother Teresa gave me her personal written permission to share her words and teachings in this book. I chose my favorite lessons, which came from her own lips and pen. Many of these lessons of love were spoken and written directly to me, and many were spoken and written indirectly to us *all*, through documentary films, letters, interviews, lectures, and other books. For this reason, in addition to thanking Mother Teresa herself, I wish to express my sincere appreciation to the following authors, publishers, and filmmakers for their kind permission to share selected material in this book:

Ahern, Bishop Patrick V. *Maurice & Thérèse:Story of a Love*. Doubleday, 1998.

Columbia magazine. "Remembering Mother Teresa." November 1997.

Cunningham, Frank, editor. *Words to Love By*. Based on interviews by Michael Nabicht and Gaynell Cronin. Ave Maria Press, 1983.

Delaney, John J. *Saints Are Now*. Doubleday, 1981.

Doig, Desmond. *Mother Teresa: Her People and Her Work*. Fount Paperbacks, 1978. © Nachiketa Publications, 1976.

Egan, Eileen. *Such a Vision of the Street*. Doubleday & Company, Inc., 1985.

Gonzalez-Balado, José Luis. *In My Own Words*. Liguori Publications, 1996.

— *Mother Teresa: Always the Poor*. Liguori Publications, 1980.

— *Stories of Mother Teresa: Her Smile and Her Words*. Liguori Publications, 1983.

—, editor and Janet N. Playfoot. *My Life for the Poor: Mother Teresa's Life and Work in Her Own Words*. Harper & Row, 1985.

Goodwin, Jan, "A Week With Mother Teresa," *Ladies Home Journal*, May, 1984.

Hunt, Dorothy, editor. *LOVE: A Fruit Always in Season*. Ignatius Press, 1987.

LeJoly, Edward, S.J. *Mother Teresa of Calcutta: A Biography*. Harper & Row, 1977, 1983.

Lewin, Ted. Mother Teresa Illustration, *Family Circle* Magazine, April 1980.

Moorhouse, Geoffrey. *Calcutta*. Hold, Rinehart & Winston, 1971.

Muggeridge, Malcolm. *Something Beautiful for God: Mother Teresa of Calcutta*. HarperCollins, © 1971 by the Mother Teresa Committee.

Petrie, Ann and Jeanette. *Mother Teresa*. The acclaimed film documentary, Petrie Productions, Inc., 1986.

Rai, Raghu and Navin Chawla. *Faith and Compassion — The Life and Work of Mother Teresa*. Element Books, 1996.

Scolozzi, Brother Angelo Devanada, arrangement. *Total Surrender*. Servant Publications, 1985.

Serrou, Robert. *Teresa of Calcutta: A Pictorial Biography*. McGraw Hill Book Company, 1980.

Spink, Kathryn. *Mother Teresa of Calcutta: The Authorized Biography*. HarperCollins, 1997.

— *Life in the Spirit: Reflections, Meditations, Prayers*. Harper & Row, 1983.

— *The Miracle of Love*. Harper & Row, © 1981 by Colour Library International Ltd., reprinted by permission of HarperCollins.

Stern, Anthony, arrangement. *Everything Starts From Prayer: Mother Teresa's Meditations on Spiritual Life for People of All Faiths*. White Cloud Press, 1998.

Mother Teresa: *A Gift for God: Prayers and Meditations*. Harper & Row, 1975.

— *The Love of Christ: Spiritual Counsels*. Harper & Row, 1992.

Saint Thérèse of Lisieux. *Story of a Soul*. ICS Publications, 1975, 1976.

Saint Thomas à Kempis. *The Imitation of Christ*. Viking Penguin, Inc., © Leo Sherley-Price, 1952.

Time magazine. "Seeker of Souls." September 15, 1997.

Tower, Courtney, "Mother Teresa's Work of Grace," *Reader's Digest*, December 1987.

Women's Day magazine. A selection of Mother Teresa's moving and inspirational words. Dec. 19, 1989.

About the Author

Susan Conroy made her first trip to Calcutta to work with Mother Teresa and the Missionaries of Charity in 1986. In 1987, at the request of Mother Teresa herself, Susan spent two weeks in the Order's convent in the South Bronx, New York, in contemplation of the religious life. During these two weeks, a time she calls "the most profoundly meaningful experience of my life," Susan came to know Saint Thérèse of Lisieux, who has had as great an impact on Susan's life as Mother Teresa. Susan did not enter the Order, but in 1991, during Lent, she once again returned to Calcutta to work with the Sisters among the dying destitutes. She and Mother Teresa kept up

Author Susan Conroy and her niece, Abigail Marie Joy, 2002.

their correspondence until Mother's death in 1997. Today, in addition to her work as a tax specialist, Susan translates the works of Saint Thérèse of Lisieux from French into English for several publishing houses. *Mother Teresa's Lessons of Love and Secrets of Sanctity* is Susan's first book.

Our Sunday Visitor . . .
Your Source for Discovering the Riches of the Catholic Faith

Our Sunday Visitor has an extensive line of materials for young children, teens, and adults. Our books, Bibles, booklets, CD-ROMs, audios, and videos are available in bookstores worldwide.

To receive a FREE full-line catalog or for more information, call **Our Sunday Visitor** at **1-800-348-2440**. Or write, **Our Sunday Visitor** / 200 Noll Plaza / Huntington, IN 46750.

- -

Please send me: __A catalog
Please send me materials on:
__Apologetics and catechetics   __Reference works
__Prayer books   __Heritage and the saints
__The family   __The parish
Name_____
Address_____Apt._____
City_____State_____Zip_____
Telephone (   ) _____

A33BBABP

- -

Please send a friend: __A catalog
Please send a friend materials on:
__Apologetics and catechetics   __Reference works
__Prayer books   __Heritage and the saints
__The family   __The parish
Name_____
Address_____Apt._____
City_____State_____Zip_____
Telephone (   ) _____

A33BBABP

- -

OurSundayVisitor

200 Noll Plaza
Huntington, IN 46750
Toll free: **1-800-348-2440**
E-mail: osvbooks@osv.com
Website: www.osv.com